50
Early Childhood Literacy Strategies

JANICE J. BEATY

Elmira College, Emerita

PEARSON

Merrill
Prentice Hall

Upper Saddle River, New Jersey
Columbus, Ohio

Library of Congress Cataloging-in-Publication Data

Beaty, Janice J.
    50 early childhood literacy strategies / Janice J. Beaty.
        p. cm.
    Includes bibliographical references.
    ISBN 0-13-118154-8 (paper-spiral bound)
        1. Language arts (Early childhood) 2. Early childhood education—Activity programs. 3.
    Picture books for children. I. Title: Fifty early childhood literacy strategies. II. Title.

LB1139.5.L35B42 2005
372.6–dc22   2004044552

Vice President and Executive Publisher: Jeffery W. Johnston
Publisher: Kevin M. Davis
Editor: Julie Peters
Editorial Assistant: Michelle Girgis
Production Editor: Sheryl Glicker Langner
Design Coordinator: Diane C. Lorenzo
Cover Design: Jim Hunter
Cover Image: Corbis
Production Manager: Laura Messerly
Director of Marketing: Ann Castel Davis
Marketing Manager: Autumn Purdy
Marketing Coordinator: Tyra Poole

This book was set in Optima by Carlisle Communications, Ltd. It was printed and bound by Courier
Kendallville, Inc. The cover was printed by Coral Graphic Services, Inc.

Photo Credits: All photos courtesy of Janice J. Beaty

Pearson Education Ltd.   Pearson Education Australia Pty. Limited
Pearson Education Singapore Pte. Ltd.   Pearson Education North Asia Ltd.
Pearson Education Canada, Ltd.   Pearson Educación de Mexico, S.A. de C.V.
Pearson Education–Japan   Pearson Education Malaysia Pte. Ltd.

10 9 8 7 6 5 4 3 2 1
ISBN: 0-13-118154-8

Preface

Here is the answer to the early childhood teacher's familiar dilemma: **what to do about teaching literacy to young children.** *50 Early Childhood Literacy Strategies* presents an easy-to-use, easy-to-understand approach involving young children's own emergence into the world of reading and writing. Teachers and student teachers will quickly learn what picture books and activities to use with children, how to use them, and how children can benefit from their use. They will learn what to expect as young children's writing emerges from scribbles, to pictures, to real words. And finally they will come to grips with the concept of *emergent literacy* as it appears in preschool children and evolves into *conventional literacy* as it is taught in elementary school.

Our ideas on how children learn to read and write are continuing to change as advances in neuroscience give us new understandings of the human brain mechanisms underlying reading. This text takes advantage of this new knowledge by presenting strategies that speak to the way children learn. These strategies are tied to the ordinary contents and activities of the early childhood classroom, i.e., books, blocks, chalk, crayons, computer, cooking, dolls, dramatic play, easel painting, finger painting, flannel boards, hammering, puppets, scissors, singing, and storytelling. But the contents and activities are given a "literacy twist" that helps teachers set them up for children's development of early reading, writing, listening, and speaking.

Each strategy begins with a literacy concept that briefly but concisely explains the topic. At the heart of each strategy are the practical literacy activities to be used with children, often involving hands-on story activities, drawing, writing, singing, and pretending with character dolls, toy animals, and themselves. The theme throughout the text focuses on **words:** hearing words, speaking words, writing words, and reading words—the basis of early literacy. At the same time, the strategies focus on **children** and what they can do to develop these literacy skills. There are more than 50 ways.

Each young child comes to the literacy table as an individual who joins the feast at different times, at different levels, and with an appetite appropriate only to him- or herself. With 50 different dishes set before them, children and teachers too can pick and choose what works best for them. Good appetite!

KEY FEATURES

- Strategies are arranged alphabetically for easy selection. On the inside covers is a table of the strategies grouped by category.
- Most of the strategies are tied to children's picture books at the early childhood level. More than 200 of the finest books have been selected and described or listed within the strategies.
- The activities described have been chosen as models for your easy use, as well as to emulate with your own ideas.
- Assessment of children's literacy progress can be partially accomplished with the following developmental checklists: Book Handling Behaviors, Developing Eye-Hand Coordination with Cooking Tools, Early Childhood Writing Behaviors, Independent Skills, Reading Behaviors, Speaking Behaviors, and Caption Writing Progress.

USING THIS BOOK

50 Early Childhood Literacy Strategies can be used by itself as a handy activities book by teachers, student teachers, and volunteers. It can also be used in any early childhood methods and materials course, children's literature or language course, or any reading or literacy course. College students especially appreciate activity books like this for use in their student teaching or practicum experiences. In addition, it can be used as a supplement to early literacy textbooks such as the author's *Early Literacy in Preschool and Kindergarten* (with L. Pratt), or other textbooks by the author such as *Skills for Preschool Teachers* and *Building Bridges with Multicultural Picture Books.*

ACKNOWLEDGMENTS

I want to thank my editor, Kevin Davis, for his encouragement and support; Dr. Linda Pratt, Executive Director of the Elmira College education program, for being the "godmother" of this text; Ann Gilchrist, director of the Central Missouri Foster Grandparents program, for allowing me to work with and film the wonderful grandparents working in Head Start programs in central Missouri; Sheryl Langner, production editor, for her special talent in making textbooks attractive; and the following programs and parents for allowing me to photograph their children: Park Avenue and Fay Street Head Starts in Columbia, Fulton, and Mexico, Missouri; Walnut Creek Day School, Columbia, Missouri; Noah's Ark Preschool in Taos, New Mexico; and Arnot Museum Nursery School in Elmira, New York. Also I wish to thank the following programs for sharing children's writing samples and artifacts: Park Avenue Head Start, Columbia; Walnut Creek Day School, Columbia; the Missouri Association for Community Action calendar art for 2003; and especially entries for 2004 from Head Starts in Carrollton, Fredericktown, Independence, Marble Hill, Park Hills, Springfield, St. Louis, and St. Joseph, Missouri.

Contents

Children's Picture Books
(Listed or Described)

*muilticultural

A, My Name Is Alice
Abiyoyo*
Abuela*
Alphabet Under Construction
Amazing Grace*
Angel Child, Dragon Child*
Apple Farmer Annie
Astronauts Are Sleeping
Arthur's Adventures with D. W.
Aunt Flossie's Hats*
B Is for Bulldozer: A Construction ABC
Baby-O!*
Beach Feet*
Beastly Feast, The
Beasty Story, A
Bein' with You This Way*
Bigmama's*
Blueberries for Sal
Bringing the Rain to Kapiti Plain*
Brown Bear, Brown Bear, What Do You See?
Building a House*
Bunny Cakes
Caps for Sale
Carlo Likes Reading
Carlos and the Squash Plant*
Cat Count
Cat in the Hat, The
Charley Parker Played Be Bop*
Chicka Chicka Boom Boom
Cleversticks*
Click, Clack, Moo: Cows that Type
Close Your Eyes
Cock-a-Doodle-Do!*
Corduroy*
Counting Crocodiles
Crazy Hair Day
Curious George
Curious George Rides a Bike
Dancing with the Indians*
Diary of a Worm
Dinosaurumpus
Do Donkeys Dance?
Dogs in Space
Dora's Backpack*
Doorbell Rang, The
Down by the Cool of the Pool
Down by the Station
Drat that Fat Cat
Dr. Seuss's ABCs
Duck in a Truck
Dumpling Soup*

D. W.'s Guide to Preschool
Eat Your Peas, Louise
Edward the Emu
Eleanor, Ellatony, Ellencake, and Me
Families Are Different*
Famous Seaweed Soup
Farmer in the Dell, The
Feast for 10*
Feathers for Lunch
Fiddle-I-Fee
Fire Fighters
Five Little Monkeys Jumping on the Bed
Flower Garden*
Francis the Scaredy Cat
Froggy Goes to the Doctor
Giggle, Giggle, Quack
Gingerbread Baby
Gingerbread Boy, The
Giraffes Can't Dance
Going to the Zoo
Goldilocks and the Three Bears
Good Morning Franny, Good Night Franny*
Good Night Moon
Green Eggs and Ham
Grinch Who Stole Christmas, The
Haircuts at Sleepy Sam's*
Hammers, Nails, Planks, and Paint
Handa's Surprise*
Homemade Love*
How Do Dinosaurs Say Goodnight?*
Hue Boy*
Hush!*
I Am Me*
I Am Not Sleepy and I will Not Go to Bed
I Can Do It Too!*
I Can't Said the Ant
I Know a Rhino
I Love My Hair*
I Love You: A Rebus Poem
I Went Walking
I Will Never Not Ever Eat a Tomato
I'm a Little Teapot
I'm Calling Molly*
I'm Gonna Like Me
If You Give a Moose a Muffin
If You Give a Mouse a Cookie
If you Give a Pig a Pancake
If You Take a Mouse to School
If You're Happy and You Know It!
Incredible Me
Isla*

Addresses of Educational Supply Companies

Childcraft Education Corporation
PO Box 3229
Lancaster, PA 17604
(1-800-631-5652)
www.childcraft.com

Constructive Playthings
13201 Arrington Rd.
Grandview, Missouri, 64030
(1-800-448-4115)
www.cptoys.com

Demco Reading Enrichment
PO Box 7488
Madison, WI 53707
(1-800-356-1200)
www.demco.com

Lakeshore Learning Materials
2695 E. Dominguez St.
Carson, CA 90810
(1-800-778-4456)
www.lakeshorelearning.com

Library Video Company
PO Box 580
Wynnewood, PA 19096
(1-800-843-3620)
www.LibraryVideo.com

Scholastic, Inc.
2931 E. McCarty St.
Jefferson City, MO 65101
(1-800-724-6527)
www.scholastic.com

Weston Woods
143 Main St.
Norwalk, CT 06851
(1-800-243-5020)
www.scholastic.com/westonwoods

Discover the Companion Website Accompanying This Book

THE PRENTICE HALL COMPANION WEBSITE: A VIRTUAL LEARNING ENVIRONMENT

Technology is a constantly growing and changing aspect of our field that is creating a need for content and resources. To address this emerging need, Prentice Hall has developed an online learning environment for students and professors alike—Companion Websites—to support our textbooks.

In creating a Companion Website, our goal is to build on and enhance what the textbook already offers. For this reason, the content for each user-friendly website is organized by topic and provides the professor and student with a variety of meaningful resources. Common features of a Companion Website include:

For the Professor—

Every Companion Website integrates **Syllabus Manager**™, an online syllabus creation and management utility.

- **Syllabus Manager**™ provides you, the instructor, with an easy, step-by-step process to create and revise syllabi, with direct links into Companion Website and other online content without having to learn HTML.
- Students may logon to your syllabus during any study session. All they need to know is the web address for the Companion Website and the password you've assigned to your syllabus.
- After you have created a syllabus using **Syllabus Manager**™, students may enter the syllabus for their course section from any point in the Companion Website.
- Clicking on a date, the student is shown the list of activities for the assignment. The activities for each assignment are linked directly to actual content, saving time for students.
- Adding assignments consists of clicking on the desired due date, then filling in the details of the assignment—name of the assignment, instructions, and whether or not it is a one-time or repeating assignment.
- In addition, links to other activities can be created easily. If the activity is online, a URL can be entered in the space provided, and it will be linked automatically in the final syllabus.
- Your completed syllabus is hosted on our servers, allowing convenient updates from any computer on the Internet. Changes you make to your syllabus are immediately available to your students at their next logon.

For the Student—

- **Introduction**—General information about the topic and how it will be covered in the website.
- **Web Links**—A variety of websites related to topic areas.
- **Timely Articles**—Links to online articles that enable you to become more aware of important issues in early childhood.
- **Learn by Doing**—Put concepts into action, participate in activities, examine strategies, and more.

- **Visit a School**—Visit a school's website to see concepts, theories, and strategies in action.
- **For Teachers/Practitioners**—Access information you will need to know as an educator, including information on materials, activities, and lessons.
- **Observation Tools**—A collection of checklists and forms to print and use when observing and assessing children's development.
- **Current Policies and Standards**—Find out the latest early childhood policies from the government and various organizations, and view state, federal, and curriculum standards.
- **Resources and Organizations**—Discover tools to help you plan your classroom or center and organizations to provide current information and standards for each topic.
- **Electronic Bluebook**—Paperless method of completing homework or essays assigned by a professor. Finished work can be sent to the professor via email.
- **Message Board**—Virtual bulletin board to post and respond to questions and comments from a national audience.

To take advantage of these and other resources, please visit the *50 Early Childhood Literacy Strategies* Companion Website at

www.prenhall.com/beaty

Educator Learning Center: An Invaluable Online Resource

Merrill Education and the Association for Supervision and Curriculum Development (ASCD) invite you to take advantage of a new online resource, one that provides access to the top research and proven strategies associated with ASCD and Merrill—the Educator Learning Center. At www.EducatorLearningCenter.com you will find resources that will enhance your students' understanding of course topics and of current educational issues, in addition to being invaluable for further research.

HOW THE EDUCATOR LEARNING CENTER WILL HELP YOUR STUDENTS BECOME BETTER TEACHERS

With the combined resources of Merrill Education and ASCD, you and your students will find a wealth of tools and materials to better prepare them for the classroom.

Research

- More than 600 articles from the ASCD journal *Educational Leadership* discuss everyday issues faced by practicing teachers.
- A direct link on the site to Research Navigator™ gives students access to many of the leading education journals, as well as extensive content detailing the research process.
- Excerpts from Merrill Education texts give your students insights on important topics of instructional methods, diverse populations, assessment, classroom management, technology, and refining classroom practice.

Classroom Practice

- Hundreds of lesson plans and teaching strategies are categorized by content area and age range.
- Case studies and classroom video footage provide virtual field experience for student reflection.
- Computer simulations and other electronic tools keep your students abreast of today's classrooms and current technologies.

LOOK INTO THE VALUE OF EDUCATOR LEARNING CENTER YOURSELF

A four-month subscription to Educator Learning Center is $25 but is **FREE** when used in conjunction with this text. To obtain free passcodes for your students, simply contact your local Merrill/Prentice Hall sales representative, and your representative will give you a special ISBN to give your bookstore when ordering your textbooks. To preview the value of this website to you and your students, please go to www.EducatorLearningCenter.com and click on "Demo."

ALOUD, Saying Words . . .

CONCEPT

Literacy for young children begins with speaking and listening to words and sentences. For children to become literate, they need to hear language spoken around them. They need to speak it themselves. Learning the sounds of language are keys to their later recognition of written words and letters. Teachers need to spend time daily talking to individuals about things they find interesting, and motivating other children to join in the talk. When teachers use new words, they need to point them out. When children use new words, they need to be recognized and congratulated.

Do not correct mispronounced words. Young children need to feel confident in their early stages of language acquisition. They will hear you pronouncing the words correctly and eventually copy you. Young children learn best through play. Be sure to include many word games on a daily basis. Small groups work best so that no one needs to wait long for a turn. Make **SPOKEN WORDS** the core of your literacy curriculum.

Teachers need to spend time daily talking to individuals.

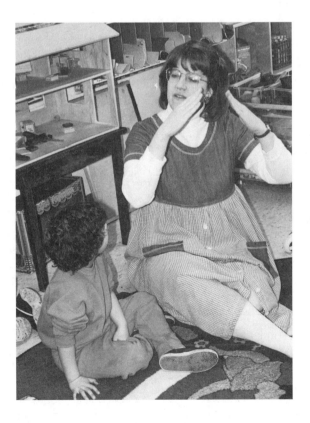

ACTIVITIES

1. "Pack Your Backpack" game. Sit in a circle with a small group and an empty backpack. Say: "I'm packing my backpack for a trip to Mars, and in it I put a _____." Make your pretend item something the children will remember, such as "a gorilla" or "a motorcycle." Then pass the backpack to the child next to you, having her repeat what you said and add a pretend something of her own. Keep the game going as long as the children can keep remembering the items and adding new things. Make positive comments on words the children use. (e.g., "A snorkel! Isn't that wonderful? Josh is going to take a snorkel to Mars! Can you tell the others what it is?")

2. "E.T. Phone Home." Sit in a circle with a small group and two toy telephones or cell phones. Pretend you are an E.T. on Earth, phoning a friend on Jupiter (one of the children in the group) to tell him what strange things you have seen on Earth. "They have boys and girls on Earth that move by walking with their feet! They don't know how to fly like we do!" Hand one of the children "on Jupiter" the phone and keep a pretend conversation going as long as he will talk. Then hand your phone to the next child and have her "phone home" from Earth to another child in the group.

3. "Snack Talk." Sit at one of the tables where children are eating their snack. After most of the snack has been eaten, choose one of the children to be the "Snack Talker" for the day. Let that child choose something interesting to talk about (not about snacks!) and begin. Children often choose topics such as their pet guinea pig, their baby sister, their new trike, or going to grandma's house. Other children can join in the conversation when the first child is finished, until everyone at the table who wants has had a turn to add to the talk. Remind them that only one child gets to talk at a time, and next day it will be _____'s turn to be the Snack Talker. You can be the model Snack Talker at first to give children the idea.

4. "Follow-the-Leader Word Fishing." Lead the class around the room, one behind the other, pretending you are the captain of a fishing boat. Use a fish net if you have one. As you walk say: "Words, words, words, words. I'm going to catch a word." As you go by the block center, pick up a toy locomotive (or bulldozer) in your net and say, "I've caught a locomotive, a locomotive, a locomotive." Have everyone behind you repeat the word out loud until you put the locomotive on a table and catch a new word, perhaps a toy dinosaur, saying: "I've caught a tyrannosaurus, a tyrannosaurus, a tyrannosaurus." When the children catch on, give the next child behind you the net and a chance to catch a new word. After everyone has had a turn, hold up each of the caught items on the table for the children to name.

CONCEPT

New brain imagery by neuroscientists has discovered that "reading relies on brain circuits already in place for language." (Shaywitz, 2003, p. 67). Teachers need to encourage children to use these language circuits before circuits for reading are in place. Thus, young children need to become aware of the sounds of words and use them repeatedly before they encounter written words.

ACTIVITIES

Wonderful word sounds can be found in books that tell cumulative stories where words must be repeated over and over each time a new object is added. You can read the story while children join in with the repeated lines.

1. Read *Down by the Cool of the Pool.* (Mitton, T., 2000, New York: Orchard Books) Each animal adds his own motion as he jumps into the pool. (Pig went wiggle, duck went flap, sheep went stamp, etc.)

2. Read *My Truck Is Stuck!* (Lewis, K., 2002, New York: Hyperion) Each vehicle that comes along gets in line to pull the truck out of a hole. (Drag and draw. Tug and tow. Engines roar. But the truck won't go.)

FIGURE 1–1 Feeling Words to Express Anger.

Mad	Incensed
Angry	Exasperated
Cross	Boiling
Upset	Fuming
Annoyed	Furious
Disgusted	Enraged
Irritated	Ready to explode
Irate	

3. Read *There Was a Bold Lady Who Wanted a Star.* (Harper, C., 2002, Boston: Little, Brown) The bold lady buys one thing after another to catch the star. (Shoes, skates, bike, car, plane, and finally rocket)

4. Read *There Was an Old Lady Who Swallowed a Trout!** (Sloat, T., 1998, New York: Holt) This Native Alaskan old lady swallows a trout, a salmon, an otter, a seal, a porpoise, a walrus, a whale, and finally the ocean before she opens her mouth and they all swim out.

5. *Use emotional words.* Other words children need to know and say out loud are emotional words from times when they are angry. The more emotional the word, the more meaningful it becomes to a child. Having children repeat emotional words aloud helps them to diffuse the emotion, but they remember the word and its sound. Children need to know as many words as possible to describe their feelings. They may not know many words that express anger. You can help by using some of the words in Figure 1–1 and helping children to say them aloud when upsetting situations occur. Feeling words can help diffuse a situation if a child says: "I am very angry about that," instead of acting out the anger by yelling or hitting.

These words not only help them express their anger but also help them feel better. Children like to use big words like these.

ACTIVITIES

Reading books about children becoming angry also helps. If you cannot acquire any of these books from a library or bookstore, make up your own anger stories or bring in a pot and have a "mean soup day," shouting angry words into the pot while stirring out the emotion.

1. Read *Mean Soup.* (Everitt, B., 1992, San Diego: Harcourt) Horace has a bad day at school, so his mother puts on a pot of water to make mean soup. For the ingredients, they shout all their troubles away into the pot until they end up smiling. You can bring in **a pot for pretend mean soup** and have upset children shout and stir words into it that tell how they feel until they feel good again.

2. Read *Sometimes I'm Bombaloo.* (Vail, R., 2002, New York: Scholastic) Katie Honor is usually a good kid, but sometimes when things do not go right she becomes Bombaloo, who shows her teeth, makes fierce noises instead of words, and throws things. What words would your children use if they were Bombaloo?

3. Read *When Sophie Gets Angry—Really, Really Angry.* (Bang, M., 1999, New York: Blue Sky Press) When her sister snatches her toy gorilla away, Sophie gets so angry she roars a red roar like a volcano. What anger words can your children roar?

4. Read *Angel Child, Dragon Child.** (Surat, M.M., 1983, New York: Scholastic) Ut, a Vietnamese girl, has a hard time at her first American school when the children use words aggressively and make fun of her. What words can your children use to help change Ut from Dragon Child back to Angel Child?

---

*Multicultural

REFERENCES

Beals, D. (1997). Sources of support for learning new words in conversation: Evidence from mealtimes. *Journal of Child Language, 24*(3), 673–694.

Cote, L. R. (1997). Mealtime in Head Start classrooms as an opportunity for literacy development. *National Head Start Association Research Quarterly,* 1, 149–155.

Kuebli, J. (1994). Young children's understanding of everyday emotions. *Young Children, 49*(3), 36–37.

Novick, R. (1999–2000). Supporting early literacy development: Doing things with words in the real world. *Childhood Education, 76*(2), 70–75.

Shaywitz, S. (2003). *Overcoming dyslexia: A new and complete science-based program for reading problems at any level.* New York: Knopf.

Vance, E. & Weaver, P. J. (2003). Words to describe feelings. *Young Children, 58*(4), 45.

2 ALPHABET

CONCEPT

Research suggests that a child's knowledge of the alphabet is one of the best predictors of her success in early reading. Does this mean you should teach preschool children the alphabet before they enter kindergarten so they will have a head start on learning to read? Not at all. Young children learn letters, numbers, and concepts of all kinds on their own by playing around with them and using them in all sorts of ways—not by being formally taught.

Teaching preschool children to memorize all the letters is not developmentally appropriate. After all, it is not the alphabet itself that children need to learn at this age, but letters from the alphabet that they find useful. As Neuman (2000) points out: ". . . long before they go to school, young children can learn to spot letters important to them, such as the "S" in Sesame Street or the "Z" of zoo" (p. 65). Often the first letter of their name is the letter they recognize first.

Self-Discovery Play

Because young children learn through play, it is useful for the teacher to recognize the levels of "self-discovery play" all children everywhere seem to progress through on their own. We call these levels "the 3-Ms of Self-Discovery": manipulation, mastery, and meaning. When children encounter new objects, say a toy telescope, they first of all **manipulate** it. They open it and close it, look through it backwards, roll it across the table, or even bang it on a pan as a drum stick.

When they finally discover how the telescope really works and what it can be used for, they pull it open, look at something through it, and close it. Then they repeat this action over and over. This is the **mastery** level, a sort of self-imposed practice. Finally, for many but not all youngsters, they progress to the

Oliver finds an "O."

FIGURE 2–1 Letters to Play with.

- **letter blocks** to transport in toy trucks
- **magnetic letters** to line up on a metal cabinet door
- **beanbag letters** to toss at a target
- **sponge letters** for dipping in paint and stamping on paper
- **lacing bead letters** to string on a necklace
- **pretzels** to break off pieces to make letters

meaning level where they make the object meaningful to them. Perhaps they go outside and look through it at a bird in a tree, or incorporate it into a dramatic play episode as a captain of a ship looking for land.

Can children play with alphabet letters like this? They can if you provide them with three-dimensional letters and give them an opportunity to experiment on their own. They may or may not use them as suggested below. They may *manipulate* them by standing them on end or piling them up. They may exhibit *mastery* by lining up the same letters over and over. They may display *meaning* by printing the letters of their name or trying to write a story.

Keep your eyes open for their own games and ideas. But don't forget to comment on what you see the children doing with the letters. "Oh, Randy, what a great tower you built out of all the 'A' blocks!" Or "Jessica, do you know what you're feeding your baby dolls? Beanbag letter sandwiches! I see a 'P' and an 'O' and a 'T.'" Or "Jake, you have stamped a 'J' on your napkin. Do you know that's the first letter of your name, J-A-K-E?"

It is up to the teacher of young children to supply the classroom with a variety of three-dimensional alphabet letters that they can play with. Remember, preschool children have not yet learned to identify many of the 26 letters by name. Activities like those shown in Figure 2–1 should help them proceed through the self-discovery play levels and identify more letters. But you also need to talk with them about the letters they are using.

Alphabet Books

Alphabet books for children of preschool age (3–5) are much more abstract than the three-dimensional letters they are playing with. This means that after reading them, you should do something playful with the letters and ideas presented by the books. The books should be bright, lively, and tell a fast-paced story if you want children to look at them. They should contain the criteria noted in Figure 2–2. Letters should stand out and be clearly related to objects that the children are familiar with.

These books present preschool children with an entirely new concept: that a letter of the alphabet represents an object. It is a concept not easily understood by young children at first, yet they do seem to memorize the fact that "A" stands for "Apple" because you say so. They may wonder "why should it?" since "A" does not look or sound anything like Apple. Remember, most preschool children are concerned with the sounds of the *names* of letters (ay), not the sound the letter makes. That will come later when they begin to recognize words.

If you have one or two alphabet books in your classroom, you should read them to one or two children at a time. Then they can sit close enough to see the pictures and begin to catch on that letters rep-

FIGURE 2–2 Choosing Alphabet Books for Preschool Children.

- One large letter to a page
- Colorful objects that children recognize
- A fast-paced story or theme that rhymes
- A lead-in to hands-on activities

resent objects or actions on the page. Later they can look at the books on their own. Use each book (not worksheets) as a lead-in to three-dimensional activities based on it.

ACTIVITIES

1. Read *Alphabet Under Construction.* (Fleming, D., 2003, New York: Holt) Mouse works his way through each huge letter on a page, airbrushing, buttoning, and carving every one. Have your listeners sit close so they can get ideas for decorating their own letters. Put out a set of white cutout letters and a basket of collage materials (buttons, sequins, tiny shells, macaroni shapes, feathers), along with colored markers and glue sticks, and have each child choose and decorate his own letter.

2. Read *B Is for Bulldozer: A Construction ABC.* (Sobel, J., 2003, San Diego: Harcourt) Read this book before or after a field trip to a construction or a road repair site. A rhyming sentence on each page shows construction equipment with their first letter in color: **C**rane, **D**ump truck, **F**orklift. Afterwards, take the book and a sheet of peel-off letters to the block building center to see if children can find any of this equipment on the block accessory shelves. Let the finder stick on its peel-off letter.

3. Read *Chicka Chicka Boom Boom.* (Martin, B. & Archambault, J., 1989, New York: Simon & Schuster) This classic story will always remain a favorite. The letters themselves talk in rhyme: "A told B, and B told C, I'll meet you at the top of the coconut tree." Then they wonder: "Chicka, chicka, boom, boom! Will there be enough room?" Children love to repeat the catchy verses and afterwards to play a game that you make up in which everyone falls down. Children can each carry a letter and march to a center spot in your room until it becomes so crowded that everyone falls down. Or you can make your own tree, wrap it in burlap, and march Velcro letters up to the top until it gets too full. Constructive Playthings (1-800-448-4115) offers a 20-inch free standing cloth tree with letters, along with a CD containing songs, rhymes, and fun.

4. Read *K is for Kissing a Cool Kangaroo.* (Andreae, G., 2002, New York: Orchard Books) Large colorful letters stand for cartoon animals doing zany things in rhyme. Children love the illustrations. Second time through the book, have the listeners find a stuffed animal in the classroom to represent a particular letter. Put the peel-off letter of its name on it. What zany things can their imaginations make it do?

REFERENCES

Beaty, J. J., & Pratt, L. (2003). *Early literacy in preschool and kindergarten.* Upper Saddle River, NJ: Merrill/Prentice Hall.

Neuman, S. B., Copple, C., & Bredekamp, S. (2000). *Learning to read and write.* Washington, DC: National Association for the Education of Young Children.

Schickedanz, J. A. (1999). *Much more than the ABC's: The early stages of reading and writing.* Washington, DC: National Association for the Education of Young Children.

Wuori, D. (1999). Beyond the letter of the week: Authentic literacy comes to kindergarten. *Young Children, 54*(6), 24–25.

3

BIG BOOKS . . .

CONCEPT

Big books are oversized paperback picture books originally made by primary teachers for the purpose of teaching conventional reading. They are used mainly in reading groups for shared reading. Sometimes students in the groups hold regular-size copies of the big book which they follow as the teacher or other students read from the big book. The large size of the books (14½ by 18 inches) makes it possible for all the students in the group to see the pictures and large print of the story as it is read aloud, and for the teacher to point out particular words and sentences. The original teacher-made big books were often traditional tales with predictable patterns of language such as *The Three Little Pigs.*

Today, commercial book publishers have reproduced numerous children's trade paperback books (the books discussed in this text) as big books, since reading programs depend more and more on children's literature rather than on traditional basal readers to teach reading. Big books with predictable stories have caught on in both elementary reading programs and more recently in preschool classrooms. (See PREDICTABLE BOOKS.)

Preschool children love to hold these giant-size books and leaf through them to look at the pictures. Teachers of young children, however, need to be aware that they will not be using big books as elementary teachers do. It is not developmentally appropriate to teach conventional reading in preschool, but instead to involve children in emergent literacy. Some teachers do read to small groups of preschool children from big books in a shared reading experience. (See SHARED READING.) Most often, however, preschool teachers get down on the same level as the children (often on the floor) and interact with them without a large book blocking their vision.

Preschool programs with limited budgets need to consider carefully how many big books they will purchase, since they are more expensive than regular-size books. It is more important for preschools to have a well-stocked library of regular children's literature picture books than a great many big books. You will want a few for the children to handle on their own, especially when you have read the same story from a regular-size book. Also, children with vision impairments may be able to see

Preschool children are intrigued by the size of big books.

the large print in the big books. Keep some big books on hand for the times you will be reading to a total group, for shared reading activities, and for children to be able to handle on their own in the book center.

ACTIVITIES

Be sure the big books you purchase are simple stories with fast action, rhyming, and repetition. Then you can get the children involved in playing word games with them. Put the big book on a stand or an easel so you have your hands free and the small group you work with can see the page and pictures clearly.

1. Read *Silly Sally*. (Wood, A., 1992, San Diego: Harcourt) Set the book on a stand or easel and gather the children around you. The children should already be familiar with the book, having heard you read the regular-size book many times (see BOOK READING). You can stand next to the book and read the first page: "Silly Sally went to town, walking backwards, upside down." Ask if any child in the group can walk *backwards* and let them demonstrate. Now each child can try. Continue turning the pages and reading until you come to the next action (i.e., dancing a jig). Ignore the "upside down" part, but ask who can *dance* a jig like the pig and have them try. Go through the entire book like this, having children look at the pictures and repeat the actions themselves. Then next time you read this big book, run your hand under the words as you read them, and ask if anyone can find the words that say "backwards," "dancing," "leaping," and so on. They have heard the words; they have demonstrated the words; now some of them may be able to find the printed words. Can anyone do it? Let them try.

2. Read *Five Little Monkeys Jumping on the Bed.* (Christelow, E., 1989, New York: Clarion) Be sure to read a regular-size edition of this book several times before you put out the big book version. Gather five children together and just as you did with *Silly Sally*, read each page, asking the five children to jump up and down where the book describes it, and having one go and sit down when the book says "one fell off and bumped his head." Next four children will be jumping, then three, two, and one. Next time through the story, ask if anyone can find a certain word on each open page, e.g., *monkeys, jumped, bumped, mama, doctor.* Make it fun, not like a test. Congratulate anyone who finds a word. Clap. If no one finds a word, you can point it out.

3. Read *Mrs. McNosh Hangs Up Her Wash.* (Week, S., 1998, New York: Harper) Read the regular-size book to the children, who will love the rhythm and rhyming on each page. For the big book version, bring in a clothes basket with several items in it as shown in the book (e.g., a dress, newspaper, stuffed animal dog, bat from *Stellaluna*, wreath, letter, apron). String a clothes line with clothespins across the back of the reading center at the children's level. Then as you read the story page by page, have one of the children pick an appropriate item out of the basket and hang it up. Next time through the story, see who can find the word on the page that names the item they have hung up.

Big Books from Scholastic (1-800-724-6527)
- *Caps for Sale*
- *Five Little Monkeys Jumping on the Bed*
- *Gingerbread Baby*
- *I Can't Said the Ant*
- *Is Your Mama a Llama?*
- *The Itsy Bitzy Spider*
- *Mama, Do You Love Me?*
- *Miss Mary Mack*
- *Mrs. McNosh Hangs Up Her Wash*

- *Saturday Night at the Dinosaur Stomp*
- *Silly Sally*
- *There Was an Old Lady Who Swallowed a Fly*
- *The Three Billy-Goats Gruff*

REFERENCES

Beaty, J. J. (1994). *Picture book storytelling*. Fort Worth, TX: Harcourt.

Cowley, J. (1991). The joy of big books, *Instructor, 101*(3), 19.

Warner, L. (1990). Big books and how to make and use them. *Day Care and Early Education. 18*(1), 16–19.

BLOCK BUILDING . . .

CONCEPT

Unit building blocks have long been one of the staple ingredients of early childhood programs. Children stack them up into towers; line them up as roads; build bridges, fire stations, hospitals, and zoos; and make corrals for their toy horses and garages for their cars. They first learn to *manipulate* blocks as two- and three-year-olds by filling up dump trucks or boxes and then dumping them out. They *master* their use by lining up rows of blocks over and over, and they finally learn to build *meaningful* structures through their playful self-discovery of the blocks. But what has this to do with literacy?

Literacy for preschool children involves speaking, listening, writing, and reading. Do children generally talk about their block-building activities? Although some builders may work in silence as they place one block on another, most children are eager, with a little encouragement, to relate what they plan to do, are doing, or have already done.

ACTIVITIES

Speaking

1. Take a photo. Take a photo of each completed block structure and ask the builders to tell you about it as you record on newsprint what they say.

2. Reporters interview builders. Have children "reporters" interview each builder for the class newsletter by speaking into a tape recorder.

3. Ask the builders. Ask the builders what they are building that they saw on yesterday's field trip to a farm, zoo, fire station, park, etc. Can they tell you a story about it? Record it on newsprint.

Listening

1. Play back the tape. Play back the tape recording of the builder's interview for the group in the block center or for individual listening with a headset.

2. Read a story. Read a story to children in the block center to motivate them to build something. Afterwards, leave the books in the block center for children to look at as they build. These or similar books are fine motivators:

> ***Going to the Zoo*** (Paxton, T., 1996, New York: Morrow)
>
> They need to listen to know what animals the book characters see. Have children get similar toy animals from the block accessory shelves; discuss with the builders how they will build enclosures for the animals and create their own zoo. Take photos.

> ***Fire Fighters*** (Simon, N., 1995, New York: Simon & Schuster)
>
> After listening to the story, have builders get out fire trucks, emergency vehicles, and plastic tubing for hoses as they learned from the story. Ask builders what they will build to house the fire trucks and what other buildings they will construct that may have a fire emergency. Take photos.

Trucks Whizz! Zoom! Rumble! (Hubbell, P., 2003, New York: Marshall Cavendish)

After reading, have builders get all sorts of trucks from block accessory shelves. Talk to them about building roads for their vehicles with toy stop signs, street signs, and maybe a bridge. Take photos.

Writing

1. Make signs for buildings. Put out pens and blank cards in the writing center for builders to make signs that identify each of their buildings in the block center. Print out the letters on a paper for children who want help in making their signs. Others may want to scribble their own signs. Mount the signs on the buildings. Take more photos.

2. Play the tape. Play the tape for the reporters who interviewed the builders for the class newsletter. Write down what each child said. Print or type out the "report" with headings. Post it on the children's bulletin board for children to look at.

3. Mount photos. Mount photos of the children's constructions in a scrapbook from the stories you have read. Have the builders dictate to you their own stories about the buildings as you write them down in the scrapbook under the photos.

Reading

1. Bring out the scrapbook. Bring out the scrapbook for the whole group to see. Ask the builders to read the stories they dictated under each photo. Most will remember the words they told you that you wrote, even though they are "reading" from memory and not from written words. Others may make up another story altogether. Accept whatever they say. It is a beginning for preliterate children.

2. Ask the reporters. Ask the reporters to "read" this week's newsletter from the bulletin board to one small group at a time. They also may be reading from memory. Each time they "read" their report to a different group, the reading process will become clearer for them. *Repetition* like this is a valuable ingredient in learning to read, just as it is in the mastery level of children's self-discovery play with new objects.

3. Ask who can read. Ask who can read the signs the builders have posted on their buildings. Have the builders tell them if they are correct (not incorrect).

4. Read the same books. Read the same books you read previously to another small group of children who would like to become the next builders in the block corner. Repeat the same activities with this group until all the children who want to have had a chance to be builders, reporters, story dictators, tape listeners, and readers.

CONCEPT

Unit blocks are also valuable for children's literacy development because of the variety of shapes they represent. Most common are the units, half units, doubles, quads, pillars, and cylinders; but there are also triangles, curves, switches, and cubes. Such blocks are stored lengthwise on low shelves so that children can see what is available and return them to their proper shelf when it is pickup time. Most teachers cut out and mount the shape of the blocks on their appropriate shelves.

Young children begin to recognize the different shapes of the blocks when it is pickup time and they must place the blocks, in order, on the shelves where they belong. At first this is difficult for some children, until they learn to match the shape of the block with the shape of the cutout or the other blocks on the shelf. Learning shapes like this is a precursor for learning the shapes of alphabet letters. Watch to see which of your children can place the blocks on the proper shelves during cleanup time.

Have children try to match blocks with shapes on shelves.

ACTIVITIES

1. Have a contest. Have a contest for several children at a time to see if they can place the blocks you set out on the correct shelves. Put out a unit, a double unit, a curve, a cylinder, and a switch. No winners or losers. Make it fun. Put out several other block shapes one at a time until each child who tries is able to match them on the correct shelves.

2. Cut white poster board. Cut white poster board into two-foot squares and invite four children to trace several different unit blocks onto their cardboards with felt tip pens. Make sure the designs they have traced are clear. Put away the blocks, put out the cardboards on a table, and challenge other children to find the blocks that fit into each tracing.

REFERENCES

Alexander, N. P. (2000). Blocks and basics. *Dimensions of Early Childhood, 28*(1), 29–30.

Cuffaro, H. K. (1995, May). Block building: Opportunities for learning. *Child Care Information Exchange,* 36–38.

Hewitt, K. (2001). Blocks as a tool for learning: Historical and contemporary perspectives. *Young Children, 56*(1), 6–13.

Hirsch, E. S. (Ed.). (1996). *The block book.* Washington, DC: National Association for the Education of Young Children.

Provenzo, E. F., & Brett, A. (1983). *The complete block book.* Syracuse, NY: Syracuse University Press.

BOOK BUDDIES . . .

CONCEPT

Book buddies are pairs of children who look at picture books together, one book at a time. They may be familiar with picture books, having been read to by parents or grandparents before they entered school, or they may be unfamiliar with picture books, having never held one in their hands until they entered your classroom. By pairing children to look at a book together during a brief period each day, children at all stages of book awareness can have the pleasure of coming together to choose a book of their liking, to learn how to handle it, and eventually to learn how to use it (i.e., demonstrate early reading behaviors). Two children together can teach each other these behaviors in an informal, fun manner that is acceptable to both.

As teachers of young children, we cannot assume that the children know how to handle a book just because they have been read to by adults. At first many youngsters may pretend to read by holding the book upside down and flipping through clumps of pages in either direction. Or they may zip through the pages, hardly noticing either pictures or text, and then slam it shut, indicating they are finished. What we do know is that "learning is developmental and acquired through social interactions." (Vygotsky, 1978). That is why starting with book buddies is important.

Choosing Picture Books

At first the books on your shelves for book buddies should be simple, fun picture books that children will want to look at and have no trouble following. Select a minimum of books to give the children a chance to see each book separately with its cover facing out on low book shelves. Putting out too many books is confusing for children and requires a longer time for each pair to select the book they want.

By becoming "book buddies," children can learn how a book works.

FIGURE 5–1 Choosing Books for Book Buddies.

- Attractive, attention-getting covers
- Large bright pictures
- Simple, brief text
- Clear sequence of episodes
- Exciting action
- Rhyme or repetition

FIGURE 5–2 Good Books for Young Children.

- *Edward the Emu.* (Knowles, S., 1998, New York: HarperCollins)
- *Handa's Surprise.** (Browne, E., 1994, New York: Scholastic)
- *How Do Dinosaurs Say Good Night?** (Yolen, J., 2000, New York: Blue Sky Press)
- *I Can Do It Too!** (Baicker, K., 2003, Brooklyn: Handprint Books)
- *Juan Bobo Goes to Work.** (Montes, M., 2000, New York: HarperCollins)
- *Noisy Nora.** (Wells, R., 1997, New York: Dial Books)
- *Silly Sally.* (Wood, A., 1992, San Diego: Harcourt)
- *Twist With a Burger, Jitter With a Bug.** (Lowery, L., 1995, Boston: Houghton Mifflin)
- *Two Cool Coyotes.* (Lund, J., 1995, New York: Dutton)
- *Whistle for Willie.** (Keats, J. E., 1964, New York: Viking)

*Multiethnic book.

Learning for young children takes time, you remember, and repetition is important. Do not be surprised if one pair selects the same book day after day. They are at the *mastery* level of self-discovery and need to try out their new learnings again and again.

The picture books you select should be geared to the early childhood level, which means they should have highly attractive covers, large bright pictures, a brief text, a clear sequence of episodes, exciting action, and words that rhyme or are repeated. Can the children identify with the characters? All the better. Be sure you choose several multiethnic books, especially from cultures present in your class, that have the attributes shown in Figure 5–1.

Figure 5–2 lists examples of books that young children are readily attracted to. Hundreds of similar books are available. But make sure the books you choose are not too long nor too complicated for the children.

ACTIVITIES

1. Send pairs to find a book. Start by sending pairs of children to find one book of their liking from the book shelves to look at with their partner. You should do the pairing at first to make sure nobody is left out. Then unobtrusively observe how much each of them knows about book handling. Take notes on what you observe each child doing and saying so you will know how to work with the individuals. Sometimes a checklist of behaviors (Figure 5–3) can help you keep track. Give the pairs a chance to look at more than one book for several days while you observe. Then sit down with the book buddies and have them show and tell you what they have found out about their books. You can do this with separate pairs or with several pairs together in a small group if it doesn't embarrass them to speak in front of others.

FIGURE 5–3 Checklist.

BOOK HANDLING BEHAVIORS

Name _____ Date_____

_____Holds book right side up in upright position

_____Opens book, cover first

_____Starts with first page

_____Turns pages one at a time, right to left

_____Looks at pictures left side first, then right

_____Knows terms: cover, page, title, author

2. Ask pair to demonstrate. Ask one of the pairs to demonstrate how she holds the book and turns the pages. Ask all of the pairs to show the others the cover of their book. Can any of them guess what the title of the book may be? Remember, most of these children are pre-readers, but some may remember the titles from your reading to the class. If they don't, you can tell them. Then ask them all to turn to the first page of their book, then the second page, the third page, and so on. Have them all go through their books slowly, one page at a time, looking at the pictures left to right. Can any of them tell what they think their book is about, or what they remember from your reading of it? Would anyone like to "picture-read" his book to his buddy? Encourage both buddies to picture-read to each other. Once again you can observe and listen.

3. Read book to whole class. In the meantime, you will be reading each of these books to the whole class, one at a time, day after day. Normally, you would read to small groups or individuals, but to get the book buddies started, it is better at first to read to the entire class, after which you can ask the buddies to select another book from the shelves and look at it together, seeing what they can find out about it. Then you will be asking each of these pairs to demonstrate the same things as before. Once you have read each of the books to the whole group over a number of days, go back and start all over, asking the group which ones they would like to hear again. Repetition like this helps the buddies become well acquainted with these particular books. Real learning takes a great deal of time and repetition.

4. Add new books. Now it is time to add new books to your original books. Five or more may be all that are needed if some of the buddies are still working with the original books. Give everyone plenty of time to get well acquainted with each of the books. You will be using them later in other literacy activities. The book buddies themselves often stay together much of the year with books they choose during free choice activities.

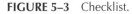

REFERENCES

Brown, D., & Briggs, L. (1992). What teachers should know about young children's story awareness. *Reading Improvement, 29*(2), 40–44.

Meier, D. R. (2000). Text strategies for literacy competency and social inclusion. In *Scribble Scrabble: Learning to read and write; Success with diverse teachers, children, and families.* New York: Teachers College Press.

Moore, L. M. (1998). Learning language and some initial literacy skills through social interactions. *Young Children, 53*(2), 72–75.

Owocki, G. (2001). *Make way for literacy! Teaching the way young children learn.* Portsmouth, NH: Heinemann.

Schickedanz, J. A. (1999). *Much more than the ABCs: The early stages of reading and writing.* Washington, DC: National Association for the Education of Young Children.

Vygotsky, L. S. (1978). *Mind in society.* Cambridge, MA: Harvard University Press.

BOOK READING . . . to Children

CONCEPT

Everyone knows children love to have stories read to them. Early childhood teachers have long included story reading as an important part of their programs. Research has finally determined that this activity is indeed essential in children's development of literacy.

Furthermore, we now know why an adult's reading aloud of stories specifically helps children learn to read by themselves. Neuroscientists have discovered that learning to read relies on brain circuits already in place for language. This means that children must use these language circuits before circuits for reading can be established. Reading stories aloud uses language circuits. Hearing stories read aloud helps children develop these circuits in the following ways:

- Children hear the sounds of the words from a book spoken aloud.
- They come to recognize these words by their sounds.
- They come to learn the meaning of these words by the book pictures that illustrate the words, as well as by the story action.
- Eventually they come to learn that these words are also represented in the book by print which they can point out.
- They come to love these books and are motivated to learn to read.

We also recognize that when children hear stories, their brains make images in their minds. These visual images promote memory development. The more frequently they hear favorite stories, the more they remember about them. Often children may correct a reader if she leaves out even one word during her rereading of a favorite book. Eventually some children are able to "read" (tell) an entire story almost verbatim from memory alone. This is one way "reading circuits" are established in the brain.

ACTIVITIES

Books that are simple, colorful, and full of exciting-sounding words are especially important to read over and over to children. Words that rhyme and words that are repeated also help children's memory development. The books listed in Figure 6–1 are among the many that contain rhyming or repeated words. (See also PREDICTABLE BOOKS.) They are available from libraries, the publishers, and educational supply compar

Reading to Children

Before Reading

1. Read book to yourself. First, you must read the book yourself looking at the cover of the book and deciding how to introduce the story, looking for interesting words or phrases to emphasize ("word tricks"), and deciding how to get the children involved in the story the second time through.

FIGURE 6–1 Paperback Books from Scholastic (1-800-724-6527).

Caps for Sale	*My Crayons Talk*
*Flower Garden**	*New Shoes Red Shoes*
*How Do Dinosaurs Say Goodnight?**	*Noisy Nora*
Is Your Mama a Llama?	*One Duck Stuck*
Madeline	*Saturday Night at the Dinosaur Stomp*
*Mice Squeak We Speak**	*Seals on the Bus, The**
Millions of Cats	*Silly Sally*
*Miss Mary Mack**	*Tikki Tikki Tembo**

*Multicultural

2. Read book aloud to yourself. Once you have made your determinations, you will need to read the book aloud ahead of time to see how it goes and how it sounds. If you wait to read it aloud until you are with the children, you may stumble over words and forget to play your word tricks.

3. Note funny incidents. For example, if you plan to start with the book *Silly Sally* (Wood, 1992, San Diego: Harcourt), you instantly notice a funny-looking, orange-haired young woman on the white cover sailing through the air upside down. Yellow flowers (buttercups) are scattered through the air and litter the yellow ground at the base of the cover. As you read through the book you see this same girl walking upside down along a path winding through a yellow buttercup field with a Medieval English town in the background. The rhyming text on the first two open pages tells you that Silly Sally went to town walking backwards, upside down. On the next two pages she meets a silly pig and they dance a jig. Then the two of them go to town dancing backwards, upside down. The story continues with Sally meeting a dog, a loon, and a sheep, and finally falling asleep. They are rescued by the forward-walking Neddy Buttercup, who tickles them all awake and they finally get to town.

During Reading

1. Introduce book to small group. You may decide to introduce the book to a small group or even two children at a time who will sit as close as possible in order to see the pictures and to participate. You begin by showing them the book cover, pointing to and saying the title **Silly Sally,** and asking

Children need to be close to the reader to see the pictures.

them what they think the book will be about. If nobody mentions "upside down," you should say the words and perhaps ask what would Sally look like if she were "right side up." Turn the cover upside down so they can see. Then read the book slowly all the way through, playing your "word tricks," but with no child participation during this first reading.

2. Play your word tricks. Your tricks could consist of "dancing" the book when the pig dances, "leaping" the book when the dog plays leapfrog, singing "la-la, la-la" when the loon sings, and snoring when they all fall asleep. When Neddy Buttercup begins his tickling to wake each one, you can reach each child and tickle him. As you might imagine, children love it and will want to have the story repeated.

3. Have children join in. Next time through, read the story as you did before, but pause after each animal's action and have the children join in when you read: "Silly Sally went to town—*dancing backwards upside down.*" Another time have the children dance, leap, sing, and fall asleep any way they can while seated. Each time you read, hold the book with the cover either right side up or upside down and ask the listeners which way the cover is and which way Sally is.

4. Use other word tricks. Using word tricks in other books you read may consist of substituting sounds for the words. For example, do a growling sound for the word "growl," a banging noise for the word "bang," or say "ah-choo" instead of "sneeze," etc. If you can't think of how to make words sound exciting, ask the children.

After Reading

1. Ask simple questions. Ask a few simple questions after the first reading to get them thinking about the story and repeating a few of its words. Which character did they like best? ("Character" may be a new word for them.) Do they remember what the pig did in the story? The dog? How did the characters eventually get to town? Talking about stories after reading them is just as important as the story itself, research tells us. Talking about the characters helps to make them real. Talking about the story helps children to understand the words they are hearing.

2. Use book as lead-in to activities. Use the book as a lead-in to other classroom activities. For instance, with *Silly Sally* some children may want to walk on their hands or do somersaults (with your assistance) on a mat in the large motor area. Others may want to do easel painting in yellow and purple about Sally and her adventures. Others may want to play with cut-out characters (see CHARACTER CUT-OUTS) on a road they build in the block center. Be sure to put the book out for the children to look at in whatever center they are using at the time. *Silly Sally* is a funny book. Make it fun for your children by following the sequence shown in Figure 6–2.

FIGURE 6–2 Reading Books to Young Children.

1. Choose simple, colorful books with exciting-sounding words.
2. Read the book yourself, silently and then aloud.
3. Introduce the book by showing children the cover.
4. Read to individuals or a small group, showing them the pictures.
5. Use "word tricks" by making actions or sounds for book words.
6. During repeat readings, have children participate by saying exciting words, phrases, or making motions.
7. After reading, ask children what they liked about the characters or story.
8. Use book as a lead-in to other classroom activities.

REFERENCES

Beaty, J. J., & Pratt, L. (2003). *Early literacy in preschool and kindergarten.* Upper Saddle River, NJ: Merrill/Prentice Hall.

Galda, L., & Cullinan, B. (2000). Reading aloud from culturally diverse literature. In Strickland, D. C., & Morrow, L. M., *Beginning reading and writing.* New York: Teachers College Press.

Neuman, S. B., Copple, C., & Bredekamp, S. (2000). *Learning to Read and Write: Developmentally appropriate practices for young children.* Washington, DC: National Association for the Education of Young Children.

Shaywitz, S. (2003). *Overcoming dyslexia: A new and complete science-based program for reading problems at any level.* New York: Knopf.

Wood, A. (1992). *Silly Sally.* San Diego: Harcourt.

7 BOOK TAPES, VIDEOTAPES . . .

CONCEPT

Young children learn to speak by listening to the language spoken around them. They learn to read, at least partly, by listening to stories read to them. Research tells us that reading aloud to children is *the single most important activity for building the understanding and the skills essential for reading success* (Neuman, et al., 2000). Thus we know how significant listening to stories is in the process of becoming literate.

The hands-on reading of a book to a child does make a difference. This is the first thing that must happen before any use is made of the technology currently surrounding books: a human being must first read the actual book to the child—again and again. Young children learn best through active participation with hands-on activities and human interaction, not by sitting and listening to a mechanical device. Using computer programs, book tapes, or book videotapes should come *after* children have had the initial experience of having a favorite book read to them over and over by a person.

Book tapes and videotapes do have a role to play in helping children learn to read. Although they are more abstract than the actual reading aloud by a person, nevertheless they can help children develop listening skills, memory skills, and a better understanding of a story they are already acquainted with. As long as book films, audiotapes, and videotapes are not substituted for the actual reading of books or the telling of stories by people, they can be used in their own special way.

In addition to helping children better understand stories, book media can also help them understand "book language," the language of literature, which is different from the conversational language they hear spoken around them. They hear new words, new phrases, longer sentences, and new ways to use words. For children with a hearing impairment, book media can be a life-saver if turning up the volume will help them. For children learning English as a second language, book audiotapes and videotapes can be played over and over until they get the words and their pronunciation right.

ACTIVITIES

Book Videos

The use of book videos is somewhat different than many adults might suppose. Videos should not be in the early childhood classroom for the children's entertainment but for children's learning. Before using book videos, teachers need to read the actual book to small groups, then discuss the story and pass the book around for children to see for themselves. Whenever a book video is played, the teacher should be present with the book itself in hand to show children that the video is a story that comes from the book she is holding and that they may look at by themselves.

1. Review the videotape by yourself before using it with children. Is the tape the same as the story in the book? Is there a place in the story where you can stop the tape and ask the children to respond to a question? You may want to find out if they can really follow the story sequence by asking: "What do you think will happen next?" Or something about a character: "Why do you think Grace gets upset after she is chosen to play Peter Pan?" (from *Amazing Grace*). Or if they remember

21

how the story ends: "How do dinosaurs really say goodnight?" You do not have to respond to the children's answers by telling them whether they are right. Instead, say: "Let's look at the rest of the video to see how the story turns out." Now you have created an interactive learning experience, not just an entertainment.

2. Use the TV for book videos only. When the video is finished, turn off the television and put the video away unless children with special needs have a use for it. Make sure the television is used only for short book videos like this. Whenever a TV is present in the classroom, there is always the temptation to turn it on for the children to watch other programs. Instead, your program itself should be an exciting time for children to become involved in lively activities, not passive sitting and watching.

3. Put book in the book center or listening center. Have the book being shown available in the book center or listening center for children to look at afterwards, perhaps making comparisons with the video.

4. Put out book props for every book video you show. Children enjoy playing with the characters from their favorite books. (See CHARACTER DOLLS.) Pretending with character dolls makes the stories come alive for them. Children's own creativity is stimulated when they make up their own scenarios for the characters. Commercial dolls are available for several of the videos listed below: Curious George, Grace, Llama, Strega Nona, Willie, Pooh, Joseph. Other props can include colored caps for re-enacting *Caps for Sale,* plastic dinosaurs, magnetic alphabet letters, a toy saxophone, and plastic farm animals. Or you can make your own character cutouts from duplicated pages of the books. Book videos may be borrowed from some public libraries or you can purchase them from companies such as the Library Video Company. Their large selection includes many of the books discussed in this text and the popular titles shown in Figure 7–1.

Book Tapes

Book tapes or audiocassettes, on the other hand, can help young children develop listening and pre-reading skills—but only if the book is also available for the child's use while the tape cassette is being played. If it is your goal to bring children and books together, it is important to understand that a book tape alone cannot perform this function. Children need to be able to see the actual pages of a real book as they hear the story being read or the tape played. Because they are still not able to read the words, they need to learn when to turn the pages of the book when they hear a page-turning signal. Thus they are also learning how a book works, another important pre-reading skill.

FIGURE 7–1 Videotapes from Library Video Company (Phone: 1-800-843-3620).

Adventures of Curious George	Noisy Nora
Amazing Grace*	Stand Tall, Molly Lou Mellon
Blueberries for Sal	Story, A Story, A*
Caps for Sale	Stone Soup
Chicka Chicka Boom Boom	Strega Nona*
Click, Clack, Moo: Cows that Type	Tikki Tikki Tembo*
Cook-a-Doodle-Doo	When Sophie Gets Angry
Dr. Seuss' Green Eggs and Ham	Whistle for Willie
How Do Dinosaurs Say Goodnight?*	Why Mosquitoes Buzz in People's Ears*
Is Your Mama a Llama?	Winnie the Pooh
Leo the Late Bloomer	Yo! Yes?*
Mama, Do You Love Me?*	

*Multicultural

1. Have several headsets. Headsets are essential for each child to enjoy a personal listening experience, as well as for keeping the recorded story from disturbing the others. Several children can listen at once if you have several headsets connected to a multi-headset board or jackbox and to the recorder. This means you will need several copies of the book that is being played. The reduced price of paperback books makes it possible for most programs to order several copies of favorite books.

2. Help children use book tapes on their own. Children can be encouraged to listen to book tapes on their own, as long as a teacher checks to see how they are doing it. Show them how to use the equipment, putting in the tape or CD. Show them how to open the book to the first page and get started with the tape. Tell them how to turn the page every time they hear the page-turning signal. At first they may have trouble keeping up with the recording by not turning the page at the proper time. You may need to listen along, without the headsets, to model the page-turning routine. Once children are on their own, check back from time to time to see if they are keeping up with the story by turning the pages.

3. Make your own book tapes. You can produce your own cassettes for books that have none available. Simply record your careful reading of the book onto a blank tape. As you turn each page, make a page-turning signal such as tapping a glass with a spoon. Listen to your tape with a headset to make sure it is clear and expressive. If not, do it over until it sounds right to you.

4. Keep books and tapes together. Many, but not all children enjoy listening to book tapes and operating the equipment. Keep paperback copies of the books in a clear plastic bag along with the tape. Do not put out all of your tapes and books at once, but mainly those you have previously read to the children. Then keep a record of which children listen to which books. Do they finish the tapes? Some children do not. Encourage them to stay with the tape until the end. You can follow along on a copy of the same book, helping them turn the pages when it is time. Find time to talk with them about their listening. What tapes do they like the best? Do they listen to the same story over and over? Oftentimes children who listen to particular book tapes will want you to read them the same book. Repetition like this is important in the learning-to-read process. The Library Video Company sells "audiobooks" (i.e., a cassette and book package) that include many of the books discussed here and listed in Figure 7–2.

5. Play Book Tapes and Videos in Different Languages. Weston Woods (1-800-243-5020) offers another fine collection of:

> book videos (V),
>
> book/cassettes (BC), and
>
> book/CDs (BCD) in several languages. You may not have
>
> French (VF),
>
> Japanese (VJ),
>
> Mandarin (VM), or

FIGURE 7–2 Audiobooks from Library Video Company (Phone: 1-800-843-3620).

Amazing Grace*
Bigmama's*
Charlie Parker Played Be Bop*
Click, Clack, Moo: Cows that Type
Itsy Bitsy Spider, The
Joseph Had a Little Overcoat*
Knots on a Counting Rope*
Strega Nona*
Thunder Cake
Tikki Tikki Tembo*

*Multicultural

FIGURE 7–3 Multiethnic Selections from Weston Woods (1-800-243-5020).

Amazing Grace (BC, BCD, V, VF, VJ, VM)

Caps for Sale (BC, BCD, V, VM)

Click, Clack, Moo: Cows that Type (BC, BCD, V, VS)

Curious George Rides a Bike (BC, BCD, V, VS)

Leo the Late Bloomer (BC, BCD, V, VS)

Noisy Nora (BC, BCD, V, VS)

A Story, a Story (BC, V, VM)

Strega Nona (VC, VCD, V, VF, VJ, VM, VS)

Whistle for Willie (VC, VCD, V, VM, VS)

FIGURE 7–4 Spanish Collection from Weston Woods.

Cuentos para crecer (includes *Leo the Late Bloomer, Owen*, and *Chrysanthemum*)

La gallinita roja (includes *The Little Red Hen, Stone Soup, Why Mosquitoes Buzz in People's Ears*, and *Charlie Needs a Cloak*)

Jorge, el monito ciclista (includes *Curious George Rides a Bike, Millions of Cats, Noisy Nora*, and *The Snowy Day*)

Max, el prodigio musical (includes *Musical Max, Monty, Whistle for Willie*, and *Panama*)

Spanish (VS) speaking children in your class; nevertheless, English-speaking children very much enjoy seeing and hearing videos of their favorite books spoken in another language. If any children come from one of these cultures, this is the time to invite family members to participate in book reading and storytelling—in their home language, if they agree. Figures 7–3 and 7–4 offer titles for such opportunities.

Would the children like to learn some words from another language? Ask the youngsters how they would like to use these book cassettes, CDs, and videos. You may be surprised at the creative approaches they suggest.

REFERENCES

Beaty, J. J., & Pratt, L. (2003). *Early literacy in preschool and kindergarten.* Upper Saddle River, NJ: Merrill/Prentice Hall.

Collins, N. L., & Schaeffer, M. R. (1997). Look, listen, and learn to read. *Young Children, 52*(5), 65–68.

Jalongo, M. R. (2000). *Early childhood language arts.* Boston: Allyn & Bacon.

Neuman, S. B., Copple, C., & Bredekamp, S. (2000). *Learning to read and write.* Washington, DC: National Association for the Education of Young Children.

Okagaki, L., & Diamond, K. E. (2000). Responding to cultural and linguistic differences in the beliefs and practices of families with young children. *Young Children, 55*(3), 74–80.

CHANTING . . .

CONCEPT

Chanting is "any group of words that is recited together with a lively beat" (Buchoff, 1994). When young children chant they speak together in unison, and as they do they learn the importance of clear and expressive pronunciation of words. Chanting involves rhyming words and repetition, as well as a catchy rhythm that takes hold of the listener and won't let go. Most advertising jingles, cheers at sporting events, and jump-rope rhymes are forms of chanting everyone recognizes.

Because children love to recite chants over and over, they learn to say unfamiliar words just for the effect they produce when they rhyme. The rhythm and rhyming helps them to remember the words and the chant itself. Chants help pave the language circuits in the brain for using new words the children will eventually learn to read. Even children who speak nonstandard English and those who are learning English as a second language love to chant, and their copying of what the group is chanting helps them learn the standard language.

ACTIVITIES

Because emerging successfully into literacy is such an important goal in most preschool programs, many teachers look for chants in the picture books they will be reading to the children. Then the children who learn to chant along with the teacher's repeated readings will be drawn to look at the books themselves: yet another motivation for learning to read. A number of new books as well as old favorites can be read for the chants they contain.

1. Read *The Lady with the Alligator Purse.* (Westcott, N., 1988, Boston: Little, Brown) Here is a traditional jump-rope rhyme with each verse ending with the catchy:

> Call for the doctor,
>
> Call for the nurse,
>
> Call for the lady with the alligator purse.

In this case Tiny Tim swallows the bathtub water and soap, but when the doctor calls for penicillin and the nurse calls for castor oil, the lady opens her purse and out pops pizza. So be ready to have a pizza party. Afterwards, have children make up their own stories about different characters and what happens when the doctor comes. Can they do them as chants?

2. Read *Dinosaurumpus.* (Mitton, T., 2002, New York: Orchard Books) Children's attraction to dinosaurs will certainly be satisfied with this book since it is all in rhymes which make fine chants. A new dinosaur enters on every page, demonstrating his steps. Children can join in the chant at the end of each page and later become the dancing dinosaurs themselves.

> Shake, shake, shudder,
>
> Near the sludgy old swamp,
>
> Everybody's doing the dinosaur romp.

3. Read *Miss Mary Mack.** (Hoberman, M.A.; 1998, Boston: Little, Brown) Here is another classic chant children love to recite. In this case Miss Mary Mack, Mack, Mack, all dressed in black, black,

Everyone chants a jump rope rhyme.

black ends up jumping the fence for fifty cents every day with the elephant. It is important for you to follow up children's favorite chants like this with some of your own. Chants can be used to tell time, give messages, or give directions that children follow with glee.

> Pick up the blocks, blocks, blocks;
> Don't watch the clocks, clocks, clocks;
> Put all the books, books, books,
> Back in their nooks, nooks, nooks,
> Put on your jacket, jacket, jacket;
> Don't make a racket, racket, racket;
> Walk down the hall, hall, hall,
> And that is all, all, all.

Physical Movements to Chants

Wait until children have learned the chants by heart before you add physical responses. Soon they will all want to clap as they call out the chant. Clapping to a beat is an important rhythmical accomplishment that not every preschool child learns immediately. Have them practice by clapping out each child's name according to the syllables. Brenda would be clap-clap; Melissa:clap-clap-clap; Urius Thompson: clap-clap-clap—clap-clap.

Once children can clap to simple chants, have them march around the room saying the chant and clapping at the same time. Some picture books show people moving or dancing to the beat of a chant. After they know the chants they can foot stamp or toe-tap while seated, when standing, or while moving along. Such actions help to develop the physical coordination also needed for learning to read and write.

4. Read *Rap A Tap Tap: Here's Bojangles—Think of That!** (Dillon, L., & Dillon, D., 2002; New York: Blue Sky Press)   In colorful silhouette-like cutouts, Bojangles taps through every double page of this book as he joyfully dances his way across city streets in rhyming verse. The one-sentence text at the bottom of every left-hand page is followed by the chant: "rap-a-tap-tap—think of that!" on the right-hand page. Have your children join in the chant right away. Then have them clap the chant and foot-tap the chant. Soon they should be able to rap-a-tap-tap around the room in a follow-the-leader line as you read the book.

———————
*Multicultural book

5. Read *Twist with a Burger, Jitter with a Bug.** (Lowery, L., 1995, Boston: Houghton Mifflin) Another book children can't seem to leave alone is this wonderful jig-sway-polka-twist story in which colorful multiethnic cartoon characters "dance to a mambo, snap to a rap, put on their cleats and tap, tap, tap." Children love to "rattle in their bones up a dark, dark street" in hats of every description, with walking sticks, and wearing colored scarves. The whole group can call out the chant while one or two children demonstrate the actions; or all the children can form a conga line around the room with everyone chanting and dancing.

Buchoff advices: "Give children opportunities to experiment with the rhythm and tempo of the chant, and encourage them to try different actions. By varying the response, children have the opportunity to recite the same chant multiple times but with novel approaches" (p. 29).

Patterned Chants

Some picture books are written in verses that do not necessarily rhyme but follow a rhythmic pattern. Research shows that patterns like these help the brain process and understand new information. Chanting, like singing, is thus a perfect pre-reading tool for helping children understand language patterns before symbolic codes (words) are introduced (Snyder, 1997).

Such research also helps us understand why children who have learned nursery verses, jump-rope rhymes, and chants are more successful later on in learning to read. Some researchers believe that all brain processing seeks and stores patterns of behavior that help the brain process and understand new information. The following book is written in a patterned chant that children delight in repeating.

6. Read *Bein' with You This Way.** (Nikola-Lisa, W., 1994, New York: Lee and Low)   A sprightly African American girl leads a line of multiethnic children through a park, checking out and comparing the arms, legs, nose, eyes, and hair of everyone they see in a rap-like chant that ends each description with another chant. Have your children join in: "Isn't it incredible, Simply unforgettable, Bein' with you this way!" Words such as hair, eyes, nose, arms, and skin are repeated in a pattern rather than in a rhyming chant. But it is the catchy rhythm that makes everyone want to clap hands or move to the beat. If you cannot acquire this book through inter-library loan or other sources, make up your own chants.

REFERENCES

ity, J. J, & Pratt, L. (2003). *Early literacy in preschool and kindergarten.* Upper Saddle River, NJ: Merrill/Prentice Hall.

Buchoff, R. (1994). Joyful voices: Facilitating language growth through the rhythmic response to chants. *Young Children, 49*(4), 26–30.

Cole, J. (1989). *Anna Banana: 101 jump-rope rhymes.* New York: William Morrow.

Davies, M. S. (2000). Learning . . . the beat goes on. *Childhood Education, 76*(3), 148–153.

Snyder, S. (1997). Developing musical intelligence: Why and how. *Early Childhood Education Journal, 24*(3), 165–171.

---

*Multicultural book

9   CHALK, CRAYONS . . .

CONCEPT

Chalk

Drawing implements such as chalk can also become writing implements when the time is right. Young children emerge into writing through experimenting with all sorts of tools: paintbrushes, pencils, pens, markers, chalk, crayons, sticks, and even their fingers. But even before they use chalk for writing, many young children begin to draw pictures with it. Often they are drawing to tell a story, still another way chalk can lead children into literacy.

It is important not to push children into representational drawing before they have satisfied their drive to explore the medium. (Oken-Wright, 1998). First of all they need to learn on their own how chalk works. When young children first pick up a piece of chalk (make sure it is a thick one), they tend to play with it, moving it lightly or scribbling it firmly all over a chalkboard, the sidewalk, or the paper you provide. They are engaged in the *manipulation* level of self-discovery play. They need to work their way through this initial experimentation before you can expect them to draw a picture or write a letter.

You will know when they have finally "got the hang of it" when they repeat the same scribbles or designs over and over. They have progressed to their self-imposed practice level we call *mastery*. Finally, they arrive at *meaning* when they begin to put meaning into their drawings. (See ALPHABET.) If you push children to draw what you want them to draw, or ask them to tell you what they have drawn, you may short-circuit their self-exploratory play and discourage them from continuing.

Drawing eventually leads to talking and writing, so be sure to give children plenty of time to explore the medium of chalk before you ask them to talk. If you observe what children are doing with chalk from day to day, you should be able to determine how they are progressing through the levels of manipulation, mastery, and meaning.

ACTIVITIES

1. Grocery bag drawing. Start with a small group of children, no more than five or six. Give them each a thick piece of white chalk and a large piece of cardboard, a large brown grocery bag, brown wrapping paper, or a place at the chalkboard if you have one. Also provide each with an eraser or sponge for erasing their work. Have them "experiment with their chalk" to see what it does and what they can do with it.

2. Paper roll drawing on floor. Some will want more paper when theirs gets "too messed up." You may want to start with a large roll of brown wrapping paper which you unroll across the floor if you have no chalkboard. Children love to work on the floor. Make sure there is plenty of room for everyone in the group. Bring in a cassette recorder and put in a music tape that will play softly as they work.

3. Talking about drawings. Choose your own comments about the children's chalk drawings carefully. To ask them "What is it?" is not appropriate, for they will be engaged in a process, not a picture. Even comments such as "Tell me about your drawing" may not elicit a real answer because there is nothing to tell, or they may make up something just to please you. Better to use words of encouragement such as: "I like the way you're holding the chalk today, Heather," or "You certainly worked hard with your chalk today, Keshawn," or "You filled the whole paper today, Amber. Good for you." Oken-Wright suggests that a better open-ended question for eliciting a response may be: "What's happening here?" (p. 78).

4. Listening to children's comments. Eventually some of the children may want to talk about what they are drawing because they have progressed to the meaning level in their exploration. Listen to what they are saying to each other as they draw. Some children may declare their intention of what they plan to draw before they start. Others pick up their ideas from one another and talk about their drawings as they work on them. Still others may be willing to talk about their drawings to the group when they are finished.

5. Working in small groups. Working in small groups like this, where everyone sees what the others are doing and shares ideas, helps the entire group to progress in drawing and talking skills. Because chalk is a temporary medium that can be erased easily, even the shyest child will be encouraged to try it.

6. Chalk storytelling. Now you can start your "chalk talking" sessions on a daily basis. Does anyone have a story to tell about his drawing? This can be the beginning of children's storytelling in your class, an important precursor to story reading for children.

Yolanda stands at the chalkboard and draws her story as she tells it. She talks about her family, telling about her mother, father, brothers and sisters, the new baby, and her gerbil. You can tape-record Yolanda's story, if she agrees, and print it for her in the book she is making, where she can illustrate it again with colored chalk, markers, or crayons.

7. Sidewalk drawing. If your children enjoy drawing with chalk, there are several other chalk experiences they should try. *Sidewalk chalk* can be used outside on a sidewalk or driveway, but be sure to get permission first. Many children like to squat down to draw with thick pieces of white or colored sidewalk chalk on a surface that is much grainier than chalkboards or paper. Their drawings tend to spread out across the walk. They may or may not want to talk about them. Often there is no story attached, but simply chalk scribbles flowing down the walk. But some children may take a literal point of view and tell a story about a character walking down the sidewalk as they draw.

8. Wet paper or wet chalk drawing. To keep colored chalk drawings from rubbing off the paper, sheets of high quality paper can be moistened with a sponge before children draw on them, or liquid starch can be sponged on the paper to keep it moist and provide a better finish. Instead of wetting the paper, the colored chalk itself can be soaked in a solution of sugar water (1/3 cup of

Yolanda tells her story as she draws it.

sugar to 1 cup water) for five minutes before use to increase the brilliance of the colors. As the chalk dries out, it can be dipped in the sugar water.

9. Chalk writing. Most initial scribbling that young children do with chalk eventually turns into representational drawing, as previously mentioned. But some of the scribbles can also become early writing. Children often recognize that teachers write words under their pictures, so they pretend to do the same with horizontal scribble writing. This kind of writing is discussed under Strategy #15, Early Writing, and Strategy #31, Pictures, Caption.

CONCEPT

Crayons

In some programs, the use of crayons has been minimized in favor of colored markers. Children may find the markers easier to use, but they should not neglect crayons entirely because of their important role in strengthening the finger muscles necessary for holding writing tools. Cherry (1972) reminds us: "The child can practice moving his arm, wrist, and lower palm rhythmically on a table top or floor, as he pushes a crayon back and forth and round and round. This prepares him for writing where similar, but more controlled, motions are necessary" (p. 46).

Large kindergarten-size crayons are preferable for the youngest children who use the whole hand for gripping. They need to be waxy, but hard enough to resist breaking. Young children tend to bear down hard when drawing with crayons, often breaking the regular-size ones. As children develop the fine motor control of their fingers and fingertips, they can handle the regular crayons more effectively. Keep crayon colors separated in jars or baskets so children can learn to identify the particular colors they want to use. It is not necessary to put out all the colors at once. Six or eight large crayons are enough for an individual to start with.

Young children's initial experiences with crayons are similar to that of chalk. They begin by manipulating them, scrawling marks and scribbles up and down and around. Keep baskets of crayons available on the art shelves so that children can get plenty of practice scribbling with crayons. Large sheets of paper on the floor or on the tables help children learn to control these drawing/coloring tools. Eventually they will start drawing pictures and naming them. Be accepting of anything the child draws whether or not it looks like the object she names.

ACTIVITIES

Crayon Talking

Crayons, like chalk, can also involve children in telling stories about their crayon scribblings or drawings. You can initiate the process by reading a book like:

1. Read *My Crayons Talk.* (Hubbard, P., 1996, New York: Henry Holt) Here is an outlandish book of colors with a funny, crayon-drawn girl on every page telling what her giant crayons say. For instance, "purple" shouts: "Yum! Bubble gum!" with a purple bubble ballooning from her mouth. What can your children's crayons say? Crayon talking seems to come more easily if you unroll a roll of white paper across the floor, as you did for the chalk, and have children from a small group get down on the paper, far enough apart to have *plenty* of room to draw. Everyone can see what everyone else is doing and may copy if they wish, but it will be in their own unique style. Keep unrolling the paper as children keep expanding their drawings. "What's happening here?" "Does anyone have a story to tell?"

2. Crayon talking at wall runner of paper. Another day mount a long runner of paper on the wall like a chalkboard for the children to fill with scribbles and designs. Those who want can do "crayon talking" here, just as they did standing at the chalkboard.

FIGURE 9–1 This is mama sunflower and her baby seeds.

Mama sunflower and her baby seeds

3. Crayon scribbling. Do children also evolve into scribbling letters with crayons? Yes. By the time they are doing representational drawings and making up stories, they may also make horizontal scribbles under their drawings to stand for writing. Some children, of course, will print real letters. (See EARLY WRITING.)

4. Crayon story illustration. Children enjoy making their own illustrations of favorite books. During a science project of planting seeds, one teacher read the book, *Planting a Rainbow* (Ehlert, L., 1988, San Diego: Harcourt), about planting flower seeds and watching them grow into a rainbow of colors. Children made their own flower and seed books, dictated a story, and illustrated it with crayon drawings. Figure 9–1 is one.

REFERENCES

Beaty, J. J., & Pratt, L. (2003). *Early literacy in preschool and kindergarten.* Upper Saddle River, NJ: Merrill/Prentice Hall.

Cherry, C. (1972). *Creative art for the developing child.* Belmont, CA: Fearon.

Healy, L. I. (2001). Applying theory to practice: Using developmentally appropriate strategies to help children draw. *Young Children, 56*(4), 28–30.

Oken-Wright, P. (1998). Transition to writing: Drawing as a scaffold for emergent writers. *Young Children, 53*(2), 76–81.

CHARACTER DOLLS, CUTOUTS

CONCEPT

Before most young children can "emerge into reading" at the preschool level, they need to develop a "sense of story"–that stories are plotted narratives in which characters act in certain ways and events take place in a sequence. The youngest children do not view stories from picture books that way at first. They tend to treat each page of the book as a separate unit, not part of a continuing narrative. The more experience children have with picture book stories and their characters, the more aware they become of this narrative flow.

The more familiar children become with the characters in their favorite stories, the more they begin to make sense of this narrative structure. To make their sense of story even stronger, some teachers have children pretend to be their favorite characters and act out the story. (See STORY RE-ENACTMENTS.)

Another effective way to bring stories and book characters alive is through the use of character dolls or character cutouts. After all, one of the reasons children come to love certain books is because they can identify in some way with the characters. If they can actually play with their favorite characters outside of the book, they will even be able to create their own narratives.

Character Dolls

Just like popular children's movies that result in a whole host of commercial character action figures, certain children's picture books also have their own character dolls available in children's book stores and from educational supply houses. Named dolls come with some of the books. Generic dolls can be purchased from educational supply houses. Educational supply houses also have storytelling kits that include character dolls (Figures 10–1 and 10–2).

FIGURE 10–1 Dolls from Childcraft Education Corp. (1-800-631-5652).

African American doll, Jamaica & Anglo doll Kristin from *Jamaica's Find**

African American doll Linda from *Masai and I**

Jack doll from *Jack and the Beanstalk*

Red Riding Hood doll from *Little Red Riding Hood*

Goldilocks doll from *Goldilocks and the Three Bears*

Mrs. Honey doll from *Mrs. Honey's Hat*

Old lady doll from *There Was an Old Lady Who Swallowed a Fly*

Grandpa and girl dolls from *Shoes from Grandpa*

Hawaiian girl doll Marisa from *Dumpling Soup**

Hispanic doll Rosalba from *Abuela**

*Multicultural

FIGURE 10–2 Dolls from
Demco, Reading Enrichment
(1-800-356-1200).

Arthur & D. W. dolls from *D. W.'s Guide to Preschool*

Cat in the Hat doll from *The Cat in the Hat*

Grinch doll from *The Grinch Who Stole Christmas*

Dora the Explorer doll from *Dora's Backpack**

Ms. Frizzle doll from *The Magic Schoolbus*

Curious George monkey doll from *Curious George*

Mouse doll from *If You Give a Mouse a Cookie*

Wild things dolls from *Where the Wild Things Are*

Goose puppet from *To Market, To Market*

Lyle doll from *Lyle, Lyle, Crocodile*

Penguin doll from *Tacky the Penguin*

Madeline doll from *Madeline**

Olivia doll from *Olivia*

Dear One doll from *Mama, Do You Love Me?**

Grace doll from *Amazing Grace**

Mrs. Honey doll from *Mrs. Honey's Hat*

MacDonald doll from *Old MacDonald Had a Farm*

Peter and Willie dolls from *Whistle for Willie**

Young Peter doll from *The Snowy Day**

Bat doll from *Stellaluna*

*Multicultural

ACTIVITIES

It is important to keep these dolls separate from the baby dolls in the dramatic play center. These are character dolls from books and need to be kept and played with the book when it is in use. How will you use them with children to help them become involved in the stories?

1. Read *One of Three.** (Johnson, A., 1991, New York: Orchard Books) This is a story of three "steppingstone" sisters in New York City—Eva, Nikki, and me—who do most things together: walk to school in the rain, play hopscotch on the sidewalk, sit outside the bakery and smell the good smells, ride on the subway with their mama, and hold hands in the store so they won't get lost. But sometimes the little narrator of the story, me, gets left behind with her artist parents when her older sisters go out. She doesn't like it at first until she becomes "one of three" with Mama, Daddy, and me.

Read this story to a small group with three of the children holding generic African American character dolls. Make sure they all see the realistic illustrations of the book characters. Afterwards ask the three which character they have chosen to be. What would they like to do on their pretend walk around the classroom "city"? When they return to the reading circle, have their dolls tell what they saw. Did any of them see construction workers building a huge tower? Servers setting a table in the "restaurant"? Or did they only talk about children in the block center and children setting the table in the house corner?

2. Re-read story having different characters. Read the story again and have three different children become the sister characters who walk through the classroom "city." Tell them to use their imaginations. Another day, ask one of the characters if her doll can tell the story of *One of Three* or make up her own story.

Children can have their doll characters tell the story.

CONCEPT

Cultural Characters

Be sure to read many books with child characters from different cultures so that your children can come to know these cultural characters by identifying and bonding with them. They will learn about how children like themselves from diverse cultures play, work, eat, dress, and go to school; and how they feel, act, and even "act out." Such cultural book characters provide an especially effective way for children to get to know children from different cultures.

Children seem to have no difficulty choosing these cultural characters as role models. They enjoy the characters in their storybooks and, if the story appeals to them, they want to hear it again and again. They want to play with and pretend with the character doll. Whether the culture being read about is represented in the classroom makes no difference. All children can celebrate any culture on a daily basis by looking at and listening to cultural character picture books and playing with the character dolls.

ACTIVITIES

1. Paper doll cutouts. What if your program does not have the funds to purchase such dolls? You can make your own as "paper-doll cutouts" simply by cutting out pictures of favorite characters from the dust jacket of the book or from an inside illustration that you print out on a color duplicator. Laminate the cutout, trim it, and mount it on a Styrofoam base. Some children prefer to play with these character cutouts rather than dolls. Make whole families of character cutouts and children can make up their own stories, perhaps using buildings in the block center or a dollhouse as their characters' houses.

As you look for picture books for your children, try to find some with characters your children may want to emulate and whose adventures they may want to experience. Today they can be characters from more cultures than ever before. Children who are involved with the characters of the books they love will also come to understand what stories are about, want to hear more of them, and want to make up some of their own.

Cultural character cutouts help bring stories to life for young children.

REFERENCES

Beaty, J. J. (1997). *Building bridges with multicultural picture books.* Upper Saddle River, NJ: Merrill/Prentice Hall.

Beaty, J. J., & Pratt, L. (2003). *Early literacy in preschool and kindergarten.* Upper Saddle River, NJ: Merrill/Prentice Hall.

Pratt, L., & Beaty, J. J. (1999). *Transcultural children's literature.* Upper Saddle River, NJ: Merrill/Prentice Hall.

Whitney, T. (1999). *Kids like us: Using persona dolls in the classroom.* St. Paul, MN: Redleaf Press.

Zeece, P. D. (1997). Bringing books to life: Literature-based storytelling. *Early Childhood Education Journal. 25*(1), 39–43.

11

CHILDREN READING BOOKS . . .

CONCEPT

When young children first begin reading books on their own, most are not reading the words. They may be reading the pictures and making up the story as they go along. Or they may be telling the words of the story from memory as they turn the pages if it is a book that has been read to them repeatedly. You should be encouraged when you observe children involved in these behaviors, for it means they are on their way to becoming real readers.

If they enjoyed the experience, children who have been read to individually soon want to read on their own. When they first look at a picture book they may not even know how it works, turning the pages haphazardly and mumbling in a jargon that sounds like an adult reading. This is *pretend reading* or *book babble.* Not all young children do it, but some of those who have been read to frequently may start out by doing pretend reading. They may pretend to read books to their friends or even to stuffed animal toys.

Eventually they will be drawn to the pictures and assume it is the pictures that tell the story in the book. Now when they read a book they may point to the pictures and name them as they tell the story still in their own words. If you listen to their *picture-naming* stories you may note that they treat each page as a separate unit and not as a part of a continuing story. They have not yet developed what reading specialists call "a sense of story," that is, 1) that stories include a sequence of incidents describing the actions of the characters, and 2) that you must turn the pages of the book to learn what happens next.

On the other hand, certain young children who have been read to a great deal at home by sitting in the reader's lap and following the pictures in a favorite book closely as the story unfolds, may be able to repeat all the words in that book almost verbatim. But she is not reading them—she has memorized

At first children think the pictures, not the words, tell the story.

them. The fact that she can "read" a whole book in the words of the author is usually so exciting to her family that they make a big fuss about it, motivating her to really learn to read words. A few children who have had a great deal of experience at home

1. by being read to,
2. by having logos and signs pointed out to them,
3. by being encouraged to draw and write stories and letters, and
4. by using the computer on their own

may enter your classroom as true early readers. You may think they have been taught to read by someone at home, but most have not. They have "emerged" naturally into reading on their own. (See EMERGENT LITERACY.)

Since you will not be teaching conventional reading to 3-, 4-, and 5-year-old children, what can you do to help as many children as possible "emerge into reading"? All 50 literacy strategies described in this book can assist you in this fascinating task, but helping children develop "a sense of story" may be as important as any of them.

ACTIVITIES

1. Read same story again and again. Children develop a sense of story (Figure 11–1) by hearing stories read to them over and over. The books themselves need to be exciting stories with easily followed plots in explicit sequences that the children can understand. They need to sit close to the reader so they can follow along.

2. Have children participate in story reading. They need to participate in the reading as much as possible by having the reader *scaffold* the reading, that is, help the child by providing a slot where the child can chime in with the words he remembers. Readers also need to ask questions about predictions such as: "What do you think will happen next?" Readers need to talk about the story afterward with the children by going over the plot sequence in fun ways. Then they need to give children the opportunity and time to look at the book on their own, and perhaps try to read it to a book buddy.

3. Read Do Donkeys Dance? (Walsh, M., 2000, Boston: Houghton Mifflin) Picture books with questions in the title are often the kind that help a beginning reader to understand that a story continues from one page to the next. In this case, the story is a simple one asking bizarre but funny questions about animals. Do pigs buzz around flowers? is the first one, with an illustration showing little pigs around a huge flower. The reader must turn the page for the answer. "No. Bees buzz around flowers." A young listener may enjoy this type of story and find it fun to answer the questions before you turn the page. Listen when she "reads" the book to a buddy to see how well she understands the story.

FIGURE 11–1 Developing a Sense of Story.

- Choose books with exciting, easily followed plots
- Read books to individual children over and over
- Help them follow the plot by asking questions, making predictions
- Talk about the plot sequence afterwards
- Give children an opportunity and time to look at the book on their own
- Encourage children to "read" the book to a buddy

4. Read *Is Your Mama a Llama?* (Guarino, D., 1989, New York: Scholastic) By now an almost classic tale, this story about the little llama who goes around asking each animal the title question has become a favorite. Steven Kellogg's whimsical full-page illustrations help carry the plot. In a rhyming cadence that helps the listener predict what's coming next, the story carries on a two-page conversation with each animal, ending with the llama predicting who the animal's mama might be. The listener can make his own prediction based on the rhyming words and pictures, and then turns the page for the answer. Reread the story as many times as your listener wants. At the end, ask him why he thinks the little llama asked all his animal friends this question in the first place. Does he understand that the llama was looking for his own mama?

5. Read *Louella Mae, She's Run Away!* (Alarcon, K. B., 1997, New York: Holt) Everyone on the farm is out looking for Louella Mae: "Has anyone seen her? Now where could she be? Go look in the hollowed-out trunk of that. . . ." The listener needs to make a prediction of what the word is that will follow on the next page before the page is turned. This story is longer than the previous ones, but rhyming words and illustrations keep a listener on the edge of his seat until the end. And what a surprise! They not only find Louella Mae, but the listener discovers who she is. Your listener will need to hear the story again and again before remembering what comes next and guessing all the answers. Its more complex plot can help a young child develop a real "sense of story." Be sure you read it to one child at a time.

6. Read *This Little Chick.* (Lawrence, J., 2002, Cambridge, MA: Candlewick Press) Here is a story for the youngest child, with striking stamped illustrations from carved vinyl showing each of the animals little chick plays with. The rhyming verse on every other page ends with a question for the listener: "And what do you think they heard him say?" He must turn the page to find the answer—always the animal sound of the particular animal chick is playing with. How long will it take your young listener to predict it correctly? It can be great fun if the listener joins in with the chick each time to make the animal sounds.

Read *This Little Chick* again to see if the listener really caught on. What does he predict that little chick will tell his mother when he gets home? Run your finger under the large-font verse and encourage him to repeat this too. Afterwards, see if he can remember which animals little chick played with and what sounds they made.

7. Read the story to book buddy. Have him "read" the story to his book buddy and unobtrusively observe how he does it. Does he still treat each page as a separate unit or does he tell a more cohesive story? The more he hears, looks at, and participates with books like this, the stronger his sense of story will become. (See PREDICTABLE BOOKS.)

You, too, will come to understand the importance of reading stories to individuals. If members of your staff cannot handle all of the reading, invite volunteers to participate (e.g., grandparents, retired teachers and librarians, Foster Grandparents Program, RSVP, AmeriCorps, or VISTA).

REFERENCES

Beaty, J. J., & Pratt, L. (2003). *Early Literacy in Preschool and Kindergarten.* Upper Saddle River, NJ: Merrill/Prentice Hall.

Campbell, R. E. (1998). A day of literacy learning in a nursery classroom. In Campbell, R. E. (Ed.), *Facilitating preschool literacy.* Newark, DE: International Reading Association.

Owocki, G. (2001). *Make way for literacy! Teaching the way young children learn.* Portsmouth, NH: Heinemann.

Schickedanz, J. A. (1999). *Much more than the ABC's.* Washington, DC: National Association for the Education of Young Children.

Sulzby, E. (1985). Children's emergent reading of favorite storybooks. A developmental study. *Reading Research Quarterly, 20*(4), 458–481.

12 COMPUTER...

CONCEPT

Does the computer have a place in an early childhood literacy program? It does. Simple computer programs based on a concept you are featuring in other learning centers can support and extend children's learning. If the program is based on a children's book, the ideas gained from the computer will be reinforced every time children look at the book.

While some teachers may view the computer with reluctance because it is a high-tech piece of equipment they themselves may not know how to use, most young children are excited to try it out with their natural "hands-on," "do-it-yourself" learning style. If you observe them, you will see them figuring it out by trial-and-error. At first everyone will want a turn. Each day, you can demonstrate to a small group the basics of how to use the computer and then let them try it on their own.

After the novelty wears off, two children at a time can choose to use the computer during the free choice period by wearing the two computer necklaces you provide. Others can "sign up" for a turn on a numbered sheet. Give computer users enough time to get deeply involved. Setting a timer for five minutes each is not enough time for real learning to take place. Onlookers can also benefit. Anderson (2000) found that children, even onlookers, spoke more when observing computer users.

Set up your computer center away from classroom traffic. It can be located in its own center, in the writing center, in the science/discovery center, or any other area where software programs support similar learning activities. Have the monitor and printer on a low table near a wall outlet so cords are kept out of children's reach. Be sure the monitor is at a child's eye level while seated and not above it. Place two child-size chairs in front of the monitor to encourage two children to interact. These pairs can learn:

- to take turns with the mouse
- to converse with one another about what they see and hear
- to teach each other how a program works
- to problem-solve together

Software Programs

Choose the software programs carefully. It is important for your literacy program that the software you choose can be integrated into the classroom learning centers (Figure 12–1). As with book tapes and videos, computer programs are more abstract than the concrete materials that are most appropriate for

FIGURE 12–1 Choosing Computer CD-ROMS.

- Tried out by teacher ahead of time
- Based on children's books being used
- Attractive to young children
- Easily used and understood by children
- Teaches appropriate skills
- Tied in to learning center activities

children's learning. But computer programs can be lead-ins to hands-on, concrete activities in the learning centers. Each computer CD-ROM should be based on a children's book you have available in the book center. It is also important that you try out the software to make sure it is at an appropriate level, contains activities attractive to the children, teaches skills you want children to learn, and can lead to hands-on activities in the learning centers.

ACTIVITIES

1. Help children become familiar with the computer.
  - how to turn it on
  - how to wait until the main menu appears
  - how to double click the mouse on the proper menu icon
  - how to wait until the program menu appears
  - how to click on the activity they wish to pursue

You will already have installed the program they are to use either by installing it on the hard drive or showing the children how to run the program by inserting its disk into the disk drive, waiting for the program menu, and clicking on a game or activity. Here is one model you can follow for many of the book/computer programs.

1. Read *Miss Spider's Tea Party.* (Kirk, D., 1994, New York: Scholastic) It is important to read this book to individuals or small groups of children a number of times so they will become familiar with it before using the computer program. Large, colorful cartoon-like illustrations on every other page show Miss Spider, a yellow garden spider, inviting various insects to her party. Two timid beetles, three fireflies, four bumblebees, six ants, seven butterflies, and nine spotted moths all refuse her rhyming invitations and flee as fast as possible. They do not want to end up as food for the spider. Finally, a little moth learns that Miss Spider wants only to be friends. He tells the other insects and they all return for the party.

2. Discuss the story with the children. Your listeners should enjoy the clever pictures of the insects and be excited to talk about the story. Does Miss Spider look scary? What about the other insects? Why are they afraid of Miss Spider? What makes them change their mind? What does Miss Spider really eat at her party? There are many new words and phrases the children will want to hear again: gloomy nook, jolly mugs, mortal dread, floral centerpiece—great sounding words. The pictures will help them learn to decipher their meanings. Now they are ready for the computer program.

3. Play *Miss Spider's Tea Party* CD-ROM. (Scholastic) Help the computer partners to sign in their names at the beginning of the program and then choose the level of difficulty of the games: easy, medium, or hard. Novice users should start with easy. Miss Spider asks the player to invite an insect to the party from the images at the bottom of the screen: ant, butterfly, bee, beetle, cricket, firefly, caterpillar and moth, or grampy spider. Players can print a guest list from the main menu to help them keep track of their progress and, when all the guests are assembled, they can print their own invitation with your help.

4. Have partners take turns playing one of the games. Each game shows an insect having trouble getting to the party until a particular problem is solved by the players. Suggest that each partner take turns playing one of the games: 1) taking the ant through a maze; 2) finding the butterflies on the flowers; 3) matching the flowers for the bees; 4) matching pairs of fireflies by the colors of their tails; 5) matching the crickets' instruments to the sounds of musical notes; 6) putting the caterpillar and moth through an obstacle course; 7) helping the beetles cross the river by jumping them onto floating leaves, tadpoles, and branches; and 8) matching grampy's photos to Miss Spider's descriptions. Listening skills, following directions, memory skills, matching skills, and eye-hand coordination are only a few of the literacy skills children will be learning as they interact with the program.

Children can interact with plastic insects after playing the Miss Spider's Tea Party *computer games.*

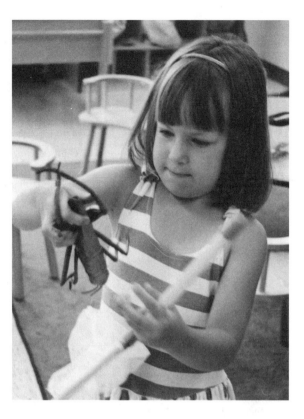

5. Participate in activities based on story. Afterwards children can carry these activities into other learning centers by counting plastic insects, starting an ant farm in the math/science center, painting insects or making play dough models in the art center, re-enacting the story in the book center, having a tea party in the dramatic play center, dictating a story in the writing center, or going outside to look for butterflies and their cocoons or chrysalises.

Another fascinating book and CD-ROM program is *Stellaluna,* very different in presentation from *Miss Spider's Tea Party.*

1. Read *Stellaluna.* (Cannon, J., 1993, San Diego: Harcourt) Although the story is longer than those in many of the picture books described in this text, children enjoy hearing it read and following the adventures of the "upside down" baby bat who falls into a bird's nest by accident and learns to live like a bird in the African jungle. The computer program focuses on the reading of the story, illustrated by wonderfully animated sound graphics. Children can choose to hear the story read, to click on objects in the scenery while the story is read, or to play a bat quiz.

2. Click on objects in the jungle scene. Words in the text are highlighted and vocalize or move when clicked on. Children often invent their own game of clicking on objects in the jungle scene (elephants, giraffe, monkey, hippo, caterpillar, moth, bats, trees) to see how many they can make move. Their partner may discover that clicking on the same object more than once results in several surprising moves. Children learn new words, word recognition, and facts about bats. They also consider the idea that animals that look very different can have the same feelings.

3. Play with African animals in block area, or with bat doll for story reenactment. Put out plastic African animals in the block area to see what kind of play ensues. A cloth bat doll can be ordered from Demco (1-800-356-1200) or children can make their own bat wings to be used in story re-enactments.

Research has determined that interactive storybook software like the sampling in Figure 12–2 is important because it offers children active participation in their own learning, consistent with the theories of Piaget and Vygotsky (Glasgow, 1996).

FIGURE 12–2 Some Software
(CD-ROMs) Based on Books.

From Constructive Playthings (1-800-448-4115)

    Chicka Chicka Boom Boom

    Curious George: Pre-K ABCs

    Miss Spider's Tea Party

From Library Video Company (1-800-843-3620)

    Arthur's Adventures with D.W.

    Curious George Preschool Learning Games

    Dora the Explorer*

    Dr. Seuss's ABCs

    Just Grandma and Me

    Stellaluna*

    Why Mosquitoes Buzz in People's Ears

*Multicultural

REFERENCES

Anderson, G. T. (2000). Computers in a developmentally appropriate curriculum. *Young Children, 55*(2), 90–93.

Beaty, J. J., & Pratt, L. (2003). *Early literacy in preschool and kindergarten.* Upper Saddle River, NJ: Merrill/Prentice Hall.

Campbell, H. (1999), *Managing Technology in the early childhood classroom.* Westminster, CA: Teacher Created Materials, Inc.

Glasgow, J. N. (1996). It's my turn! Motivating young readers. *Learning and Leading with Technology, 24*(3), 20–23.

Hutinger, P., Beard, M., Bell, C., Bond, J., Robinson, L., Schneider, C., & Terry, C. (2001). *eMERGing literacy and technology: Working together.* Macomb, IL: Center for Best Practices in Early Education.

Robinson, L. (2003). Technology as a scaffold for emergent literacy: Interactive storybooks for toddlers. *Young Children, 58*(6), 42–48.

Smith, C. R. (2001). Click and turn the page: An exploration of multiple storybook literacy. *Reading Research Quarterly, 36*(2), 152–183.

13   COOKING . . .

CONCEPT

Cooking in the early childhood classroom does not purport to teach young children how to cook. Instead, it serves as an exceptional vehicle for promoting eye-hand coordination, necessary for holding and using a writing implement, as well as for reading tie-ins with recipe charts and children's books.

Eye-Hand Coordination

To hold and control a writing implement, young children need to strengthen their arm, hand, and finger muscles. They need many experiences with hand- and finger-held objects that they must manipulate or move in certain directions. Tools used in cooking give them exceptional practice in developing this eye-hand coordination.

Observe each of the children involved in classroom cooking activities to see if he can accomplish the following tasks with cooking tools. Use a checklist like the one in Figure 13–1 or make your own. For children who have difficulty, you can demonstrate how the implement is used, give him plenty of practice, and then put him in charge of the tool if he agrees.

ACTIVITIES

1. Have children practice turning an eggbeater. Turning an eggbeater is a cranking movement that involves rotating the forearm while the fingers grip the implement's handles. Even three-year-olds can learn to operate an eggbeater, and they love to. Give them practice first with eggbeaters in the

FIGURE 13–1 Eye-hand Coordination Checklist.

**DEVELOPING EYE-HAND COORDINATION
WITH COOKING TOOLS**

Name _____ **Date** _____

_____ Turns eggbeater

_____ Turns food mill (apples, pumpkins)

_____ Stirs batter with large spoon

_____ Mixes dips with small spoon

_____ Rolls out dough

_____ Cuts with knife

_____ Scrapes carrots, potatoes

_____ Peels fruit with fingers (bananas)

_____ Dishes out food with ladle

_____ Pours liquids without spilling

FIGURE 13–2 Recipe Chart
for Oliver's Milk Shake.

Oliver's Milk Shake

1½ cups milk

½ cup crushed ice

1 banana-sliced

½ cup blueberries

Put ingredients in bowl and beat with
eggbeater until thick and frothy.

water table to let them get the knack of it. Water makes it easier without the resistance they will encounter in mixing thicker materials. You may need several eggbeaters in the water table to prevent squabbles, as this is a favorite tool.

2. Read Oliver's Milk Shake. (French, V., 2000, New York: Orchard Books) Oliver refuses to drink his milk for breakfast, so Aunt Jen takes him out to a farm to obtain the ingredients for what he comes to call his "yummy scrummy fruity frothy icy nicy tip-top tasty dreamy creamy milk shake." A small group of children at a time can make their own milk shakes using eggbeaters. Blenders are quicker, but they do not give children the small motor workout for developing the muscles needed for holding writing implements.

3. Make recipe chart for Oliver's milk shake. To make a milk shake like Oliver's, you will need 1 1/2 cups of milk, 1/2 cup crushed ice (or ice cream), 1 sliced-up banana, and 1/2 cup blueberries. Put the recipe on a newsprint chart with simple line drawings like those shown in Figure 13–2, depicting cups and fruit, along with the words in a sequence under each other.

4. Have children make milk shakes following the recipe. Have two children peel and chop the banana and put it in a bowl, two children measure and pour in the milk, one child measure and pour in the blueberries, one child measure and add the crushed ice (or ice cream). The children can then take turns beating the mixture with an eggbeater until it is thick and frothy. You may need to get it started. You can divide the ingredients into two bowls for two children to do the beating at the same time. It makes six half cups of milk shake. Children can dip out their own with a large dipper. Don't forget the straws. Now it is the next small group's turn.

5. Read Oliver's Milk Shake *to first group again.* Meanwhile, the first group can listen to Oliver's story again and compare their milk shake to his. Do they think theirs tasted as good as his? What words can they think of to describe their shake? Write down Oliver's words and see if the group can come up with tasty words for their shakes. What other kinds of fruit could they use to make a milk shake another day? Keep the picture book in the book center for children to look at for as long as they want.

6. Do milk shake activities in other areas. Would anyone like to create an artistic milk shake on the painting easel? What color paints will they need? Would the painters like to make up their own story of their milk shake when they finish, to be dictated to a teacher or spoken into a tape recorder? Some children might prefer to keep a scrapbook of their cooking activities, illustrated by their own drawings and accompanied by their own stories. For this activity, children participated in all or some of Figure 13–3's pre-writing and pre-reading skills.

FIGURE 13–3 Pre-Writing and
Pre-Reading Skills.

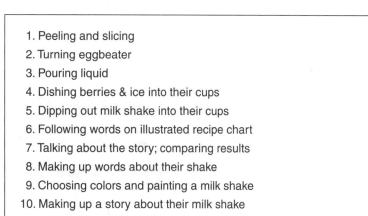

1. Peeling and slicing
2. Turning eggbeater
3. Pouring liquid
4. Dishing berries & ice into their cups
5. Dipping out milk shake into their cups
6. Following words on illustrated recipe chart
7. Talking about the story; comparing results
8. Making up words about their shake
9. Choosing colors and painting a milk shake
10. Making up a story about their milk shake
11. Drawing pictures for their stories

This activity can be continued in other areas of the classroom and into your reading of other tie-in books such as:

1. Read *Blueberries for Sal.* (McCloskey, R., 1948, New York: Viking) Little Sal goes out with her mother to pick blueberries, and little bear goes with his mother bear to do the same. What happens when they meet?

Can you take your children out to pick blueberries, or at least to a store to buy them?

2. Read *The Runaway Pumpkin.* (Lewis, K., 2003, New York: Orchard) This story is about a gigantic pumpkin that children in Halloween costumes find on top of their hill. They give it a push and down it rolls in a rhyming thumpin' bumpin' runaway pumpkin verse right into their house where grandma stirs and stews and bakes it into soup and bread and pie.

A similar activity begins with the reading of this book and ends with a cooking activity that helps children develop these same skills. It involves obtaining a pumpkin from a farm or a market, cutting it up, cooking it, running it through a food mill, and then beating it into Pumpkin Smoothies with an eggbeater, using two tablespoons of cooked pumpkin, one cup of milk, and one large sliced banana. (McKinnon, 2001)

3. Read *Apple Farmer Annie.* (Wellington, M., 2001, New York: Dutton) Annie picks all kinds of apples, using some to make sweet apple cider, smooth applesauce, muffins, cakes, and pies. Recipes at the end for applesauce, apple muffins, and applesauce cake with illustrated ingredients around the border can show your children what they need and what they need to do. Go on a field trip to pick apples if you can, or buy them from a market. After a field trip to pick apples, one class of 3- and 4-year-olds drew caption pictures for a story called "Our Adventures Picking Apples." Figure 13–4 is one.

4. Read *Warthogs in the Kitchen, A Sloppy Counting Book.* (Edwards, P. D., 1998, New York: Hyperion) Children love to laugh at the antics of the weird warthogs as three of them read the recipe for muffins, slop in 4 scoops of sugar, beat in 5 scoops of dripping butter and 6 cracked eggs (mostly on the floor), and dump in 7 scoops of flour and a pickle for good measure. Recipes for human cupcakes and warthog cupcakes appear at the end.

5. Read *To Market, To Market.* (Miranda, A., 1997, San Diego: Harcourt) If you decide to take the children shopping for the ingredients for vegetable soup, be sure to read them this book in which a lady goes to market to the traditional nursery rhyme: "To market, to market, to buy a fat pig. Home again, home again, jiggity jig!" She not only buys a pig, but also a hen, a goose, a trout, a lamb, a cow, a duck, and a goat, all of whom mess up her kitchen so that she can't cook. But when she finally collapses, they take her back to the market to buy potatoes, celery, beets, tomatoes, pea pods, peppers, garlic and spice, cabbage, rice, okra, onions, and carrots which they take home, peel, cut, slice, and chop up into a delicious vegetable soup.

FIGURE 13–4   "This is Me, Apple April, and My Cat Rosemary."

Almost any book that features foods, eating, or a particular fruit or vegetable can lead your children into exciting food preparation activities that help to strengthen their fine motor coordination as well as introducing them to new words, making up stories, and even re-enacting the adventures of the characters. (See STORY RE-ENACTMENTS.)

REFERENCES

Beaty, J. J., & Pratt, L. (2003). *Early literacy in preschool and kindergarten.* Upper Saddle River, NJ: Merrill/Prentice Hall.

Beaty, J. J. (2002). *Observing development of the young child* (5th Ed.). Upper Saddle River, NJ: Merrill/Prentice Hall.

Cosgrove, M. S. (1991). Cooking in the classroom: The doorway to nutrition. *Young Children, 46*(3), 43–46.

Dahl, K. (1998). Why cooking in the classroom? *Young Children, 53*(1), 81–83.

McKinnon, E. (2001). *Alphabet Snacks.* Grand Rapids, MI: McGraw-Hill Children's Publishing.

14 DRAMATIC PLAY . . .

CONCEPT

Dramatic play in an early childhood program is the spontaneous role-play children engage in as they pretend different real-life scenarios. Such pretend play usually takes place in the dramatic play center which is often set up with child-size kitchen furniture: sink, stove, refrigerator, cupboards, table, chairs, and all sorts of props. Teachers encourage children to pretend about family life, field trips they have taken, community events that have happened, projects they are pursuing, or stories they have listened to.

At times teachers may set up the center to serve as a supermarket, hospital, doctor's clinic, fast food restaurant, post office, beauty shop, shoe store, pet shop, fire station, laundromat, or any one of a number of real-life locations the children are familiar with. Props such as appropriate clothes, shoes, hats, purses, implements, and gear related to the roles they will be playing help children make their spontaneous dramas meaningful.

This kind of pretending is the way children make sense of their world. Whether or not such a center is available, they will pretend about events in their lives anyway: Dad starts a new job; a new baby is brought home; Grandma comes for a visit; they have to go to the doctor's for a shot. Emotional situations are especially common themes in children's pretending. Sometimes a scary television program at home prompts a new drama in the classroom. When one child put on a police hat, the other children acted uncomfortable at first, but then turned him into a police dog they could control. They built him a high-walled doghouse with the large hollow blocks to contain him. When young children are involved in dramatic play, creative solutions abound.

Where does literacy fit in? Speaking, listening, reading, and writing, the principal elements of literacy, are encouraged and supported more fully by dramatic play than by almost any other early childhood endeavor. Once children have expressed interest in a particular theme, teachers can stock the dramatic play center with literacy items. Ferguson (1999) describes a restaurant scenario in which preschoolers spontaneously pretended to read, write, and count money. Children read menus, ordered items, wrote orders, read their place mats, and paid for their food.

In every instance the children are obliged to talk to one another. This unprompted child-child conversation is one of the most important contributions of dramatic play to young children's emergent literacy. Children learn to use the words surrounding the theme they are exploring. Those who don't know the appropriate words or how to use them listen to the children who do and soon are imitating them.

ACTIVITIES

1. *Stimulate talking around dramatic play themes.*
   - Help children experience the topic first-hand through a field trip
   - Talk with the children afterwards about the field trip
   - Have children symbolize what they experienced in their drawings, singing, stories
   - Read children books about the theme
   - Provide props that will motivate pretend play about the theme

- Remain in the background unobtrusively once the play has started
- Listen, observe, and take notes on the spontaneous conversations
- Analyze the children's conversations to see what needs to happen next

2. Take children on a field trip to a medical clinic. They visited the registration area, waiting room, examining room, and x-ray room. Over the next few days they talked about what they had seen, painted pictures of it, and made and painted an x-ray machine out of a cardboard carton.

3. Read appropriate books about the theme.

- **Froggy Goes to the Doctor** (London, J., 2002, New York: Viking)
- **This Is a Hospital, Not a Zoo!** (Karim, R., 1998, New York: Clarion Books)
- **Jessica's X-Ray** (Zonta, P., 2002, Buffalo: Firefly Books)

4. Set up a dramatic play center as a medical clinic. They all wanted pretend x-rays taken of their babies' "broken arms," so the teacher helped them set up a medical clinic with a waiting area, examining table, and an x-ray area. Literacy props such as a sign-in book, telephone, and magazines were put in the waiting area. Doctor's and nurses' paraphernalia were assembled: stethoscopes, thermometers, syringes, bandages, and long-sleeve men's white shirts for lab coats. As many as six children at a time could play in this dramatic play center clinic.

5. Observe and record what occurs in this dramatic play. Conversations blossomed as children had to negotiate for the roles they wanted, sign in, wait in the waiting area, and visit the doctor to get shots for the babies or have their arms x-rayed by the technician. As children drifted in and out of the play, each group played the scenario somewhat differently. Sometimes one child would take over as the leader and assign roles: "I'll be the x-ray technician. You be the doctor. You others can bring your babies for shots and x-rays."

Everyone wanted to be the x-ray technician. The x-ray technicians in this classroom got to draw pretend x-rays (mostly lines and squiggles) on transparent sheets, and everyone wanted to do it. They had seen real x-rays on their clinic visit, as well as the ones in the book *Jessica's X-Ray.* They were intrigued with the idea of looking at bones inside the body. To make it even more realistic, the teacher brought in a little plastic skeleton from a science store. More negotiations ensued. Finally the leader gave in: "Okay. You can all be x-ray technicians who come to visit my clinic. I'll be the doctor."

Waiting for x-rays in the waiting room made some players nervous.

6. Analyze the children's conversations during their play. Staff members who listened to the clinic conversations every day recorded the following types of dialogue:

- assigning or negotiating roles (doctor): "You be the x-ray technician today."
- directing the action (x-ray technician): "No. You have to wait for your turn."
- sustaining the action (technician): "Let's go out and get more babies."
- expressing feelings (mother): "Oh, will it hurt? Don't hurt my baby."
- giving & receiving feedback (mothers; fathers): "That's not how you give a shot. You put it in there." "Where is my x-ray?" "That don't look right."
- re-negotiating roles (fathers): "It's my turn to be the x-ray man."

7. Record children's stories on tape. So much good conversation was occurring that the teacher invited players to record what happened on their visit to the clinic on a tape cassette. Later it was transcribed into a class book of "Our Visit to the Clinic" for everyone to see and hear.

8. Determine how to extend this experience. Later the teacher and staff in this classroom decided to extend the children's interest in bones with a visit to a science museum to look at dinosaur bones. They already had many picture storybooks on dinosaurs. Perhaps the children would want to "dig for dinosaur bones" in the sand table, or make model dinosaurs out of clay, or set up a dinosaur museum with their toy dinosaurs in the block center. Signs, labels, drawings, conversations, stories, and songs: all kinds of literacy activities would surely result.

REFERENCES

Beaty, J. J., & Pratt, L. (2003). *Early literacy in preschool and kindergarten.* Upper Saddle River, NJ: Merrill/Prentice Hall.

Davidson, J. (1996). *Emergent literacy and dramatic play in early education.* Albany: Delmar.

Ferguson, C. J. (1999). Building literacy with child-constructed sociodramatic play centers. *Dimensions of Early Childhood, 27*(3), 23–29.

Pellegrini, A. D., & Galda, L. (2000). Children's pretend play and literacy. In D. S. Strickland & L. M. Morrow (Eds.), *Beginning reading and writing.* New York: Teachers College Press.

Permutter, J. C., & Laminack, L. L. (1993). Sociodramatic play: A stage for practicing literacy. *Dimensions of Early Childhood, 21*(4), 13–16.

Rowe, D. W. (2000). Bringing books to life: The role of book-related dramatic play in young children's literacy learning. In K. A. Roskos & J. F. Christie (Eds.), *Play and literacy in early childhood: Research from multiple perspectives.* Mahwah, NJ: Lawrence Erlbaum.

15 EARLY WRITING, SCRIBBLING . . .

CONCEPT

Young children's first writing is scribbling. They scribble up and down and around with pencils, markers, chalk, paint brushes, and even their fingers. Most adults tend to disregard this early stage of writing, saying: "Oh, it's only scribbling." But scribbling is to writing what babbling is to speaking: an early stage of children's development that should be encouraged. As they continue to scribble, children begin to notice what they are doing. As their hands and fingers become stronger and they are better able to control their scribbling implement, their scribbles begin to evolve into shapes: circles, ovals, squares, and crosses, among others, one on top of the other.

Soon they are making scribbles that cover the middle of their paper, adding another line of scribbles underneath. This is the beginning of their differentiation between picture scribbles and writing scribbles. Sometimes they will pretend to read this pretend writing. Other times they may bring their "picture" over to you and ask you to read what it is about. Because you know how to read and they don't, they assume you will be able to translate their linear writing scribbles. Simply tell them you used to be able to read scribble writing, but now you have forgotten how. Maybe they can tell you what it says.

Their picture scribbles may eventually evolve into something like Figure 15–1, an oval "head-person" with eyes and mouth, lines of hair sticking up from the top of the oval, arm lines sticking out from either side, and two leg lines sticking down from the bottom of the oval. Balls at the ends of the lines represent hands and feet.

Their lines of writing scribbles, however, look nothing like letters or words at first. Learning to write is not only a lengthy and complex process, but it is much different from what logic tells us it ought to be. It would seem that learning to write is simply learning to make letters and combine them into words. Research has proven otherwise. Rather than mastering the parts (letters) first, children do just the opposite. They attend to the whole (written lines) first, and much later to the parts (letters) (Temple, Nathan, & Burris, 1993).

FIGURE 15–1   Here is a 4-year-old's "Head-Person" from an Apple Picking Field Trip.

Early writing is often lines of scribbles and a few mock letters.

Child development of all kinds proceeds from the general to the specific like this. In motor development, the large muscles of their arms and legs develop before the small muscles of their fingers and hands, toes and feet. In drawing, most children make generic humans who all look alike before they begin to draw specific people with identifying characteristics.

In writing, children first see the whole pattern (lines across a page) and only later can they identify separate words and finally letters. They are at the "emergent stage" in learning to write. (See EMERGENT LITERACY.) From their own observations, and not from being taught, they seem to extract the broad general features of the writing system: that it is arranged in rows across a page; that it consists of loops, sticks, and connected lines, repeated over and over. Some children fill pages of scribbled lines over and over from top to bottom in a sort of self-imposed practice, as in the 3M's "mastery" level.

Eventually you will note that alphabet-like cursive letters ("mock letters") begin to appear in their lines of scribbles. When children begin to write mostly lines of letters ("letter strings"), they may again ask you to read them, as previously noted. If given enough time and support, children will create their own knowledge about writing by extracting the information from the writing they see around them. It is not up to you to teach formal writing to preschool children. Instead, you should observe the kinds of scribble writing and mock writing they are doing and encourage them to continue by providing outlets for their writing: sign-up sheets, journals, messages, signs, lists, stories.

Printing is somewhat different from the cursive writing described here. Children also go through several emergent stages in teaching themselves to print letters and words with the letters in order. Even the letters of their names are sometimes mixed up, written backwards, upside down, or scattered around a page. The concept of a "word" is still somewhat fuzzy for them, and they often substitute the picture of an object for the word. It is not for you to correct them, but to encourage them by involving them in all kinds of writing. What they need is the freedom and time to experiment on their own. They will eventually get it right. As Temple, et al, tell us: ". . . it appears that we learn to write at least as much by discovering as by being taught. Learning to write is largely an act of discovery."

Some child development specialists are worried that teachers who are unfamiliar with the concept of emergent writing, may not know how to help these children. As Schrader and Hoffman (1986) note:

> When teachers are unfamiliar with current knowledge about the natural development of literacy in young children, they impose skill-oriented expectations and tasks on these youngsters—copying and tracing standard adult print, for example. Such activities not only are stressful for 3-, 4-, and 5-year-old children, but they do not afford children the opportunity to use their self-constructed knowledge in meaningful ways. (p. 13)

ACTIVITIES

1. Observe samples of their writing on a daily basis using a checklist. You will want to know how far along each of the children have progressed in their emergence into writing. Observe samples of their writing on a daily basis and use the checklist in Figure 15–2 to help you determine where they stand. You may find that some children skip some of the items listed while others seem to be stuck doing the same type of writing over and over (Figure 15–3). Don't forget that repetition like this is part of the natural progression and should be expected. Others may progress in an entirely different manner. Accept whatever they do and encourage them to continue in the many exciting writing activities you provide.

2. Involve children in writing activities that are purposeful but fun. Writing should be fun for these children and not a chore. But there should be a purpose behind it, as well. Some of the writing activities the children can be involved in (even if they only scribble) are shown Figure 15–4.

3. Read books in which characters are involved in writing. Also read books to small groups or individuals in which the characters are involved in writing and invite children to re-enact the stories, including the writing parts. The following books are important ones to obtain from the publishers or a library because they are simple, fast-moving, and funny enough for preschool youngsters to want to hear them again and again. Then they can choose the animal and human parts with glee for story

FIGURE 15–2 Checklist for Early Writing Behaviors.

EARLY CHILDHOOD WRITING BEHAVIORS

Child's Name _____ Age _____ Date _____

_____ Scribbles in a line across a page

_____ Scribbles in a line under drawing scribbles or a picture

_____ Fills pages with lines of writing-like scribbles

_____ Makes a few mock letters in lines of scribbles

_____ Makes more mock letters and fewer scribble marks in writing

_____ Makes printed letters here and there on a page, some reversed

_____ Prints letters of first name, but not in order, some reversed

_____ Prints first name, letters in order

_____ Prints other words along with pictures

FIGURE 15–3 Scribble Writing in a Line.

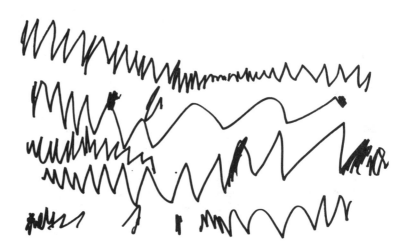

FIGURE 15–4 Authentic Writing
Activities.

Get-well cards	Signs for block buildings
Messages	Journals
Lists of ingredients	Permission slips
Lists of pets	Thank-you notes
Sign-up sheets	Stories
Birthday cards	Story (picture) captions
Mother's Day & Father's Day cards	

re-enactments as you read the words. But be sure to let Ruby, Max, and the duck print or scribble their own notes as best they can.

4. Read *Bunny Cakes.* (Wells, R., 1997, New York: Dial Books) Little bunny Max decides to make his Grandma an earthworm birthday cake. But his older sister Ruby informs him they are going to make an angel surprise cake with raspberry-fluff icing. Max tries to help but only creates a mess and is sent to the store several times with a list of ingredients to replace. Ruby carefully prints EGGS in black crayon the first time, but Max adds his own ingredients ("Red-Hot Marshmellow Squirters") as a huge red crayon scribble. The grocer gives Max eggs. When he has to return for milk, Max tries writing about the squirters in red and green, but still the grocer can't read the scribbles. In the end, Max draws a picture of two Red-Hot Marshmellow Squirters and the grocer finally understands.

5. Read *Giggle, Giggle, Quack.* (Cronin, D., 2002, New York: Simon & Schuster) Here is another hilarious Farmer Brown story. This time the farmer goes on vacation, leaving his brother Bob in charge of the animals with the warning to follow his written instructions, but to keep an eye on the duck: he's trouble. Duck finds a pencil and begins writing his own instructions for Bob about getting pizza for the hens, washing the pigs with bubble bath, and getting a video movie, "The Sound of Moosic," for the cows. When Farmer Brown calls home and hears the giggles, moos, oinks, and a quack as hen picks up the phone, he knows what has happened. Duck writes his last note: "It's for you, Bob!"

REFERENCES

Beaty, J. J., & Pratt, L. (2003). *Early literacy in preschool and kindergarten.* Upper Saddle River, NJ: Merrill/Prentice Hall.

Klenk, L. (2001). Playing with literacy in preschool classrooms. *Childhood Education, 77*(3), 150–157.

Schickedanz, J. A. (1999). *Much more than the ABCs: The early stages of reading and writing.* Washington, DC: National Association for the Education of Young Children.

Schrader, C. T., & Hoffman, S. (1987). Encouraging children's early writing efforts. *Day Care and Early Education, 15*(2), 9–13.

Temple, C.A., Nathan, R. G., & Burris, N. A. (1993). *The beginnings of writing.* Boston: Allyn & Bacon.

16

EASEL PAINTING . . .

CONCEPT

Some teachers may wonder why painting of any kind is included as a literacy strategy. Yet many aspects of child development overlap. Thus many activities that help children to develop serve several purposes. Easel painting, for example, is a highly creative pursuit. It helps children develop artistic skills and at the same time helps children to develop certain literacy skills, as shown in Figure 16–1.

For young children, art is a natural language. They emerge into painting/drawing just as they do into writing: first scribbles, then shapes, and finally pictures/letters. Easel painting is especially important for this emergence to take place because it involves the *freedom* for young children to explore and experiment on their own with the paint medium.

In the beginning they play around with brush and paint, trying to figure out which hand to use, how to hold the brush, and how to dip the brush into the paint and spread it onto the paper without dripping it all over. Their first attempts are splashes across the paper. Then as they gain control, they begin scribbling different colors on the paper, often one on top of the other, sometimes using one hand and then the other. They are not painting a picture but working through the process of learning how to paint. Once again they are progressing through the three spontaneous steps of self-discovery: *manipulation, mastery,* and *meaning.* (See ALPHABET.) Once they have learned how to manipulate this unfamiliar medium, they go on to their own self-imposed mastery by painting the same thing over and over. For some children it is merely one scribble in the center of a sheet, then the same thing on another sheet—again and again. Do not interfere. They are not "wasting paper," but practicing their new-found skill.

Eventually they progress to making scribble pictures which they may name before, during, or after they paint them. These too evolve through certain stages, as illustrated in Figure 16–2.

By now, some youngsters are also making lines of scribble writing above or below their pictures to tell the story of what they have painted. (See EARLY WRITING.) They are beginning to differentiate between scribble writing and scribble painting. Others have stumbled onto making alphabet letters with their paint brush. Thus, teachers need to be aware that easel painting can also serve as easel writing. As adults, we need to examine what words mean to us. If we think easel "painting" is for painting pictures only, we may miss altogether the "writing" many young children do at the easel.

The same concept holds true for finger painting. For some children, finger painting can also be "finger printing" or "finger writing." (See FINGER PAINTING.) As with easel painting, it is often the teacher who makes the distinction by pointing out to the child that she has made a letter. "Look, Paul. You have painted the letter "b." Can you find any other letters in your painting?"

FIGURE 16–1 Literacy Skills from Easel Painting.

- The finger strength to hold a writing implement
- The eye-hand coordination to make shapes and letters on paper with the writing tool
- The knowledge that the pictures they paint and the letters they write can communicate messages to others

1. *SCRIBBLE*
    UNCONTROLLED
    Marks made on paper for enjoyment. Child has little control
    of eye and hand movement. No pattern. 
    CONTROLLED
    Control of eye and hand. Repeated design. 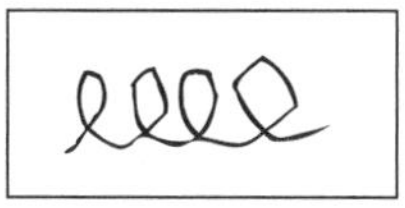
    NAMED SCRIBBLE
    Child tells you what s/he has drawn. May not be
    recognizable to adult.

2. *SHAPE AND DESIGN*
    Child makes shapes such as circles, squares, ovals, triangles.
    Child's muscle control is increasing and s/he is able to place
    shapes and designs wherever s/he wants.

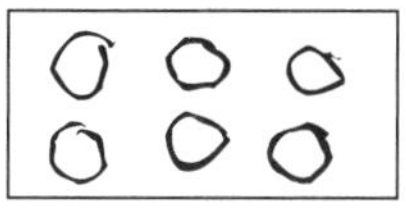

3. *MANDALA*
    Child usually divides circle or square with lines.

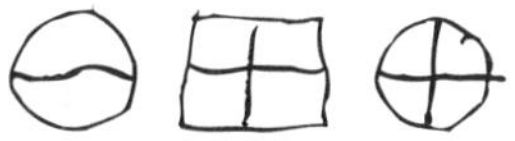

    SUNS
    Formed from oval, square, or circle with short
    lines extending from the shape. The extending
    lines take many variations.

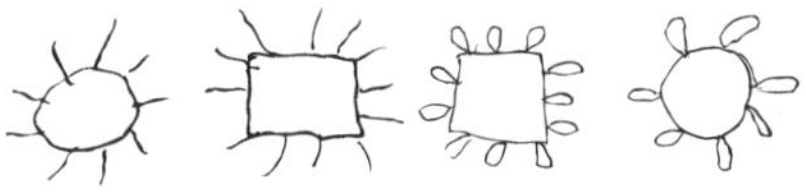

4. *RADIALS*
    Lines that radiate from a single point. Can be part
    of a mandala.

5. *HUMANS*
    Child uses SUN design and develops a face by adding
    human features. . . a "sun face."

    Child elongates several lines of the SUN design to create
    arms and legs.

6. *PICTORIALS*
    Child combines ALL stages to make recognizable designs
    or objects.

FIGURE 16–2   Stages of Art Development.

Source: From *Skills for preschool teachers* by J. Beaty, 1996, Upper Saddle River, NJ: Merrill/Prentice Hall. Reprinted with permission of B. Helm.

ACTIVITIES

1. Observe scribble painting to see if children are making letters. Observe children's scribble painting carefully to see if they are attempting to scribble write with their paint. If you see a real or mock letter within their scribble painting, point it out to the youngsters and see what other letters they can find or make. Can they do it again? Sometimes children are purposely trying to paint a letter, but often letters happen only by accident.

Four-year-old Paul has painted a "b." He may also recognize an "O" if you ask him to look for other letters.

2. Have children scribble paint their names at the bottom of their pictures. Once children evolve from the scribble stage of easel painting into the pictorial stage, painted letters usually appear only in their names at the bottom of the paper. Some children do paint a line of real or pretend writing under their pictures to tell the story. Others ask the teacher to write what they want to say about it. By now they can sign their names, even if only in scribbles.

3. Set up easels ahead of time. Set up easels ahead of time with two or three jars of liquid tempera paint and chubby brushes. Fasten large sheets of white paper to each side of the easel.

Young children need room to try out large motions with their brushes. Small sheets of copy paper are too confining. Hang as many painting aprons nearby as there are spaces to paint. As with computer chairs, it is best to have two stand-up easels next to one another so children can check on each other's work and converse about what they are doing.

4. Encourage children to talk about their paintings. Help the children use painting as a scaffold for their early writing efforts. Teachers who observe children's process over time as they paint, listen to their words, and engage them in conversations can often tell whether they are exploring the medium, trying to master it, or trying to represent something. If they have expressed an intent to represent something, you have an opening to talk with children about their pictures as they paint.

You must do it carefully. Asking "What is it?" can be an insult, when to the child it is perfectly obvious that he is painting his house. Commenting "What a beautiful picture!" does not even call for a response. Saying "Tell me about your picture" may not elicit much information either, because the child may not know what to say. Oken-Wright encourages teachers to ask instead: "What's happening here?" and indicate a specific part of the picture. This may begin a dialogue that turns into a story narrative, with the child adding to the story as she paints (p.78).

ADVANTAGES OF EASEL PAINTING

One of the big advantages of easel painting is that the easels are always there, ready to be used. By standing upright, they beckon to children to come and paint. Some teachers prefer to have children do flat painting with the easel paper laid out on tables or the floor. Although this is perfectly acceptable, easels are still more convenient for everyone involved, and a reminder to children that it's always time to paint.

REFERENCES

Beaty, J. J., & Pratt, L. (2003). *Early literacy in preschool and kindergarten.* Upper Saddle River, NJ: Merrill/Prentice Hall.

Cherry, C. (1972). *Creative art for the developing child.* Belmont, CA: Fearon Publishers.

Dyson, A. H. (1988). Appreciate the drawing and dictating of young children. *Young Children. 43*(3), 25–32.

Kane, F. (1982). Thinking, drawing—Writing, reading. *Childhood Education,* (May–June), 292–299.

Kellogg, R. (1970). *Analyzing children's art.* Palo Alto, CA: National Press Books.

Oken-Wright, P. (1998). Transition to writing: Drawing as a scaffold for emergent writers. *Young Children, 53*(2), 76–81.

17 EMERGENT LITERACY . . .

CONCEPT

Emergent literacy is the overall process for learning to read and write in a natural, self-discovery manner that begins at birth and can continue through the preschool years and into the early elementary years with proper support. Children then continue learning these skills by being taught in a conventional manner. Literacy itself encompasses the skills of speaking, listening, reading, and writing.

Circuits in the brain are already set up for infants, toddlers, and preschoolers to emerge naturally into speaking the language(s) they hear spoken around them. They do not have to be taught. But learning to read and write must be converted by young children into this language module of the brain by hearing and seeing language in its spoken and written forms. In other words, speaking is natural, but reading and writing are not. They have to be acquired. They can either emerge naturally if the circumstances are right or they have to be taught, or both.

A few young children seem to learn to read on their own from stories read to them, from computer programs they use, and from the printed material they see around them. But most children need adult assistance to involve them in appropriate literacy activities and to help them interpret what they are seeing and hearing. The natural emergence process occurs when children discover how to read and write from these activities. The conventional process of learning to read and write occurs when teachers take charge and have children follow their directions. During the preschool years, both processes are in play, but it is emergent literacy that should be encouraged whenever possible.

Reading itself consists of two major components: word identification which involves decoding, and comprehension which involves meaning (Shaywitz, 2003, p. 53). The International Reading Association (IRA) and the National Association for the Education of Young Children (NAEYC) have adopted a joint position statement on *Learning to Read and Write: Developmentally Appropriate Practices for Young Children* (1998). Included in this statement is a Continuum of Children's Development in Early Reading and Writing, shown in Figures 17–1 and 17–2.

Preschool children may function at either or both of these levels. If children are able to develop skills as they engage in these activities on their own, they are exhibiting emergent literacy. If children are taught by the teacher, they are learning through conventional teaching.

FIGURE 17–1 Phase 1: Awareness and Exploration (Goals for Preschool).

Children explore their environment and build the foundations for learning to read and write. Children can:

- enjoy listening to and discussing storybooks
- understand that print carries a message
- engage in reading and writing attempts
- identify labels and signs in their environment
- participate in rhyming games
- identify some letters and make some letter-sound matches
- use known letters to represent written language

FIGURE 17–2 Phase 2: Experimental Reading and Writing (Goals for Kindergarten).

Source: From "Learning to read and write: Developmentally appropriate practices for young children" by the National Association for the Education of Young Children, 1998.

Children develop basic concepts of print and begin to engage in and experiment with reading and writing. Kindergartners can:

- enjoy being read to and retell simple narrative stories
- use descriptive language to explain and explore
- recognize letter and letter-sound matches
- show familiarity with rhyming and beginning sounds
- understand left-to-right and top-to-bottom orientation & familiar concepts of print
- match spoken words with written words
- begin to write letters of the alphabet & some high-frequency words (p.40)

Effective early literacy instruction for preschool children includes the 50 strategies described in this text. Roskos, Christie, and Richgels (2003) have focused on eight specific strategies (Figure 17–3) that encourage early forms of reading and writing to flourish among preschool children. But they add that "Linking literacy and play is one of the most effective ways to make literacy activities meaningful and enjoyable for children" (p. 53).

ACTIVITIES

1. Make a list of all the speaking activities involving the children and you for one week. (Be specific.) Be sure to include types of child-child communication and teacher-child communication. Who initiates it? For what reason? Include story reading, storytelling, dramatic play, and block play. Include any speaking activities with phones, microphones, tape recorders, or any specific speaking setups. Decide which of these activities promotes emergent literacy, and how.

Children emerge into writing when they have opportunities to develop on their own.

FIGURE 17–3 Effective Early
Literacy Instruction.

Source: Adapted from "The essentials
of early literacy instruction" by
K.A. Roskos, J.F. Christie, and
D.J. Richgels, 2003, *Young Children,
53*(4), 53–55.

1. **Rich teacher talk**
   Use rare words
   Listen and respond to what children say

2. **Storybook reading**
   Read aloud to children once or twice a day
   Provide supportive talk before, during, and after reading

3. **Phonological awareness activities**
   Activities to increase children's awareness of sounds of
      words
   Games, poems, and songs that involve rhyme

4. **Alphabet activities**
   Alphabet books, puzzles, and magnetic letters
   Teach names of letters with personal meaning to children

5. **Support for emergent reading**
   Encourage children to read books from classroom library
   Repeated readings of favorite books

6. **Support for emergent writing**
   Encourage scribble writing, random letter strings, and
      invented spelling
   Provide a writing center stocked with materials

7. **Shared book experience**
   Read Big Books and point to print
   Read favorite stories again and again

8. **Integrated, content-focused activities**
   Children investigate topics of interest to them
   Teacher-read topic-related books

2. Make a list of all the listening activities involving the children. Include story reading and storytelling, tape or video listening, music, word sounds, animal sounds, and other specific listening activities. Decide which of these activities promotes emergent literacy and how.

3. Make a list of all the reading and pre-reading activities involving children. Tell how each activity promotes specific emergent reading skills.

4. Make a list of all the writing activities involving the children. Tell how each activity promotes specific emergent writing skills. Collect writing artifacts made by the children and tell how each demonstrates the progress of the child. Be sure to include art.

5. Compare your results in these four areas with the list in Figure 17–3. Have you included in your curriculum all of the activities listed in Figure 17–3? Are there areas where you can improve your program?

REFERENCES

Beaty, J. J., & Pratt, L. (2003). *Early literacy in preschool and kindergarten.* Upper Saddle River, NJ: Merrill/Prentice Hall.

Davidson, J. I. (1996). *Emergent literacy and dramatic play in early education.* Albany, NY: Delmar.

National Association for the Education of Young Children. (1998). Learning to read and write: Developmentally appropriate practices for young children. *Young Children, 53*(4), 30–46.

Roskos, K. A., Christie, J. F., & Richgels, D. J. (2003). The essentials of early literacy instruction. *Young Children, 58*(2), 52–59.

Shaywitz, S. (2003). *Overcoming dyslexia: A new and complete science-based program for reading problems at any level.* New York: Knopf.

18 ENVIRONMENTAL PRINT . . .

CONCEPT

Environmental print includes the signs, slogans, logos, and printed words located in the children's environment. It consists of billboards, traffic signs, fast food restaurant signs, labels on cereal boxes and food containers in supermarkets, signs on buses, slogans on T-shirts and even children's pajamas, and the many signs and labels on the items and walls of their classroom. Reading specialists have discovered that children learn to "read" this familiar printed matter seen around them on a daily basis long before they recognize the words in a book. They are, of course, memorizing these words from hearing what others call them and seeing them over and over. For many children they are an important doorway into emergent reading.

Despite the commercial aspects of some of it, outside environmental print can contribute to young children's emergent reading ability in the classroom. There seems to be more outside the classroom than inside. Xu and Rutledge (2003) point out that young children may not read the letters of the logos at first, but rely on contextual clues to help them understand the name. "For example, McDonald's familiar arch shape and golden color—and possibly its big M—create a meaningful context for children to recognize the McDonald's logo as signifying a favorite place to eat" (p.44). Using the lists in Figure 18–1, think of ways you can bring some of this print into the daily activities of the various classroom learning centers. Be sure to point to classroom signs and have them guess what they say.

Dramatic Play Center	Block Center	Science Center	Music Center
Labels on equipment	Unit blocks	Aquarium	Tape recorder
Chair Refrigerator	Trucks	Terrarium	Tapes
Table Oven	People	Pet cage	Head sets
Empty cereal boxes	Dinosaurs	Ant farm	Rhythm
Milk cartons	Animals	Collections	instruments
Food wrappers	Street signs		
Bread wrappers	Traffic signs	**Writing Center**	**Woodworking**
Hamburgers	Store signs	Computer	Saws
Magazines	Warning signs	Typewriter	Nails
Catalogs			Hammers

FIGURE 18–1   Some Classroom Environmental Print.

Even playground equipment may display environmental print.

ACTIVITIES

1. Place environmental print in the dramatic play center. Send home a note to parents asking them to look around their kitchen for words their children know, like "milk" on a milk carton, the name of a cereal they eat, or a bread wrapper. Ask them to bring these empty items to school. Collect print items yourself from your own kitchen, a fast food restaurant, as well as old magazines, toy catalogs, or a phone book. Set up a restaurant, a food store, or a kitchen in the dramatic play center, using the print items you have collected. Wrap blocks with food wrappers you have collected (e.g., hamburger wrappers, candy bar, or breakfast bar wrappers). As children play in the pretend restaurant, store, or kitchen, have them try to recognize the words of the logos.

2. Place environmental print in the block center. Take the children on a field trip outside the building and down the street. Make it a "treasure hunt" for signs. Carry a camera and take photos of the signs they see: stop signs, street names, store names, bumper stickers, gas station, directions signs (One Way), warning signs (No Trespassing), license plates, and parking signs. Enlarge the photos, cut out the signs, and mount them on cardboard for play in the block center. Or copy them on block center signs that children can use in their play. Use duplicate signs for matching games.

3. Take children on a field trip to a zoo or aquarium. Look for and copy down signs throughout the buildings and grounds, naming the animals you are looking at. Afterwards, make similar signs for the block center and encourage the children to build a zoo or aquarium for their plastic land or aquatic animals. Read books about the location you have taken them after the field trip. If the books contain signs naming the animals, see if the children can name the signs. If the books show no signs, see if your listeners can identify the sign they made for each zoo or aquarium animal when you come to the page describing the animal.

  • *Going to the Zoo* (Paxton, T., 1996, New York: Morrow)
  • *My Visit to the Aquarium* (Aliki, 1993, New York: HarperCollins)

4. Read Carlo Likes Reading. (Spanyol, J., 2001, Cambridge, MA: Candlewick), in which all the items in his bedroom are labeled with tags, as are all the items in his kitchen (which is set for breakfast); all the items in his bathroom, all the items in his living room, all the items in his playroom, all the items in his garage, all the items outside in his yard (including ants and stones), all the items on the street outside a bakery shop, all the items in the park, and all the items in a vegetable market. Obviously, your children should not be expected to name all or even many of these items. Instead, take one room at a time and see if individuals can guess the name on the label by recognizing the item. Next time you look at the story with the same children, choose a different room in the book and have them guess the names.

5. Place environmental naming signs throughout the classroom. Now it is time to begin labeling objects in your classroom. Be sure they are at the children's eye level. Have file cards cut to size, markers, and tape ready for use. Ask the first small group which five objects in the classroom should be labeled. Make your own labels and have the children stick them to the objects. Have the next groups each choose five objects they want to have labeled. The next time you read *Carlo Likes Reading,* ask the listeners to find objects in Carlo's pages with the same labels as those in the classroom. It is too confusing to put as many labels on things as in the book. It is more important for you and the children to get involved with doing the labeling and having them guess what the labels say. Otherwise they may pay no attention to the labels.

6. Match labels and objects. Some of the children may be able to match label cards from a duplicate set you have made with objects in the classroom. Put out a few label cards on a table and see if children can match any of them to the labels around the room. Make it fun.

REFERENCES

Davidson, J. I. (1996). *Emergent literacy and dramatic play in early education.* Albany, NY: Delmar.

Neuman, S. B., & Roskos, K. A. (1993). *Language and literacy in the early years: An integrated approach.* Ft. Worth: Harcourt.

West, L. S., & Egley, E. H. (1998). Children get more than a hamburger: Using labels and logos to enhance literacy. *Dimensions of Early Childhood, 26*(3 & 4), 43–46.

Xu, S. H., & Rutledge, A. L. (2003). Kindergartners learn through environmental print. *Young Children, 58*(2), 45–49.

FINGER PAINTING . . .

CONCEPT

Like easel painting, finger painting also encourages children to write as well as draw. Finger painting consists of spreading paint on paper placed on a table or floor, or directly on a desk top or tray. A child then moves the paint around with his finger, hand, arm, or a stick, making swirls, designs, or sometimes letters. The finished results on paper can be dried and displayed. Finger painting on a desk top or tray can be recovered by placing paper over it and rubbing till the paint and design adhere to the paper.

Children enjoy finger painting because it is so easy to make a mark, rub it out, and start all over. No need to pick up a brush or tool. A swipe of the hand can create a design. Another swipe can wipe it out. Experimenting with this flowing hand and finger movement gives children freedom to create an unlimited variety of forms. Some children do hand stamping in the paint. Others draw intricate designs with one finger. Those trying to master the medium may make the same swirls over and over.

A few stumble onto scribble writing and letter printing almost by accident. As Temple, et al. (1993) remind us: "Learning to write is largely an act of discovery." Once they realize they can make letters in their finger paint, some children begin making them over and over as well. Teachers may point out such letters to the children. On the other hand, most children do not differentiate writing from drawing at first.

ACTIVITIES

1. Set up finger painting. Wet the paper (finger paint paper or butcher paper is best) on both sides and place it on a smooth flat surface. One scoop of one tempera color can be heaped in the middle of the paper ready to be smeared around by the painter. Have a container of the paint and a scoop

Children sometimes make letters in their finger painting.

FIGURE 19–1 Character Stories
for Finger Painting.

Blueberries for Sal (characters: little Sal, little bear)

The Cat in the Hat (character: Cat)

Chicka Chicka Boom Boom (characters: letters, tree)

Lyle, Lyle Crocodile (character: crocodile)

Miss Spider's Tea Party (character: spider)

The Runaway Pumpkin (character: pumpkin)

Silly Sally (character: Sally or an animal)

Sometimes I'm Bombaloo (character: Bombaloo)

nearby so children can add more when necessary. Once children have become used to this sort of painting, put out two colors of paint and let them mix the colors as they paint. Because finger painting is messy, you will also need to provide painting aprons, a bucket of water, and paper towels nearby.

2. Use a variety of painting materials. Tempera paint is usually the medium of choice for finger painting, but there are other possibilities. Children enjoy variety. Once they are used to doing finger painting in tempera paint, try something different. For instance, liquid starch, liquid soap, or white paste can be used. Color it with tempera paint or food coloring. Squirting shaving cream on a tabletop also offers a fine finger painting experience. Tabletop painting gives the child more freedom since she is not limited to the size of the paper.

Another possible medium (and it is free) is mud. Children love to play in mud and should welcome the opportunity to finger paint in mud. Bring in a bucket from outside and add some liquid soap or liquid starch for transparency (Cleary, 1972, p. 104).

3. Encourage writing in the paint. Once a child has finished her painting, ask her to sign her name at the bottom. Children who have not learned how can scribble-write their names. Read a simple story with a favorite character to a small group of children before the finger painting activity. Afterwards, ask them to draw a picture of the character. Accept whatever they draw, even scribbles. Be sure they sign their names. Stories you could read might include those shown in Figure 19–1.

Children can also be encouraged to write notes, letters, or make up their own stories in finger paint. These can be dried and mounted for their authors to "read" to the class afterwards.

REFERENCES

Beaty, J. J., & Pratt, L. (2003). *Early literacy in preschool and kindergarten.* Upper Saddle River, NJ: Merrill/Prentice Hall.

Cleary, C. (1972). *Creative art for the developing child.* Belmont, CA: Fearon Publishers.

Edwards, L. C. (2002). *The creative arts: A process approach for teachers and children* (3rd ed.). Upper Saddle River, NJ: Merrill/Prentice Hall.

Ferreiro, E., & Teberosky, A. (1982). *Literacy before schooling.* Portsmouth, NH: Heinemann.

Temple, C. A., Nathan, R. G., & Burris, N. A. (1993). *The beginnings of writing.* Boston: Allyn & Bacon.

FLANNEL BOARDS . . .

CONCEPT

Flannel boards are bulletin-board size boards covered with felt or flannel used by teachers or children to tell a story with cutouts attached to them from picture storybooks. Because young children initially believe that the pictures in a book tell the story rather than the words, it is helpful to use flannel boards as yet another means for helping children develop a "sense of story."

As young children emerge into reading by hearing familiar stories read to them over and over, they begin to develop an understanding that stories flow in a certain narrative sequence. Even though they believe that the pictures in a book tell the story, they seem to treat each page of the book with its picture as a separate unit instead of as part of a whole story. Children's familiarity with a story and the pictures in the book eventually help them become aware of the narrative structure.

The use of flannel boards takes children's awareness of a story's structure one step farther. The cutout characters and events of a story are placed on the flannel board in the order of their occurrence, left to right, as the story unfolds. Someone either reads or tells the story and someone places the cutouts on the flannel board when their role is mentioned. Children listeners follow the spoken words and at the same time see cutout pictures representing these words. Thus they begin to get the feel of a story's narrative flow, a "sense of story."

Literacy specialists did not at first understand the function of pictures in helping children learn to read. They believed that deciphering words was the key in learning to read as it was taught "conventionally" in elementary school. Today many researchers now recognize that children can "emerge" into reading earlier with help from picture book pictures as a basis for establishing the meaning of the words. The realization that emergent reading can occur in preschool has brought about a renewal of interest in the use of flannel boards.

ACTIVITIES

1. Make your own flannel board. Construct a flannel board with a piece of wood, fiberboard, or heavy cardboard. The size depends on the number of children who will be viewing it. A thirty-inch square makes a large board. Some teachers make two smaller boards joined at the top and set up on a table easel-fashion. Cover the boards with flannel, felt, or suede in dark colors, and staple or glue it to the boards. Small personal flannel boards can also be made with squares of felt fastened to cardboard.

2. Order commercial flannel board storytelling figures. Commercial flannel boards are available from Lakeshore Learning Materials (1-800-421-5354) and Constructive Playthings (1-800-448-4115). They are available from Constructive Playthings for the following:

- The Gingerbread Boy
- Goldilocks and the Three Bears
- Jack and the Beanstalk
- Little Red Hen
- Little Red Riding Hood
- The Three Little Pigs

3. Create your own flannel board figures. Simple books with large pictures of the characters and a clear sequence of events are best to use. Make a color duplicate of the page showing the character

This child places cutouts of Goldilocks & the Three Bears on the flannel board as she tells the story.

or event. Cut it out and glue on a backing of felt, flannel, sandpaper, or Velcro. Then it will stick to the board but can be pulled off easily. Books discussed in this text with good sequences include:

- *Caps for Sale*
- *Edward the Emu*
- *Five Little Monkeys Jumping on the Bed*
- *Handa's Surprise*
- *Is Your Mama a Llama?*
- *Louella Mae, She's Run Away*
- *My Truck Is Stuck*
- *Silly Sally*
- *To Market, To Market*

4. Read the book to individuals or small groups. Read the book to individuals or small groups several times until they are familiar with the story and its accompanying illustrations. Then tell the story without the book, placing the flannel board characters or events on the board from left to right as the story unfolds. During the next reading or telling of the story, stop and ask the listeners "What happens next?" Then place the next character or event cutout on the board.

5. Have children volunteer to place the cutouts on the board. Now it is time for children who are interested to volunteer to be the ones to place the cutouts on the board at the appropriate time. Give everyone who wants to a chance as you read or tell the story several times. By now, one or more children may know the story and the procedure well enough to tell the story themselves and place the cutouts on the board. Put the cutouts in a labeled baggie when not in use. It is best to go over one story at a time until children know it well before introducing another flannel board story.

REFERENCES

Beaty, J. J., & Pratt, L. (2003). *Early literacy in preschool and kindergarten.* Upper Saddle River, NJ: Merrill/Prentice Hall.

Hall, N. (1998). Young children as storytellers. In R. E. Campbell (Ed.), *Facilitating preschool literacy* (pp. 84–99). Newark, DE: International Reading Association.

Schickedanz, J. A. (1999). *Much more than the ABCs: The early stages of reading and writing.* Washington, DC: National Association for the Education of Young Children.

Short, R. A., Harris, T. T., & Fairchild, S. H. (2001). Once upon a time: Telling stories with flannel boards. *Dimensions of early childhood, 29*(2), 3–9.

Van Kraayenoord, C. E., & Paris, S. G. (1996). Story construction from a picture book: An assessment activity for young learners. *Early Childhood Research Quarterly, 11,* 41–61.

HAMMERING . . .

CONCEPT

Can you drive a nail straight into a piece of wood without bending the nail or hitting your fingers? It takes well developed eye-hand coordination to accomplish this task. Such eye-hand coordination is also essential for young children to hold a writing implement and make letters in a line. Hammering gives young children one of the best kinds of practice in developing this eye-hand coordination, as well as strengthening their fingers for holding writing implements.

Using adult-size tools such as hammers would seem to be beyond the skill of such children. But it is not. Not only can they hold these tools without difficulty, they relish the challenge of doing things just like adults. Hammers in children's toy toolboxes are usually ineffective when it comes to pounding nails in wood. Medium or small adult tools are best.

Because some teachers may feel awkward using hammers and other woodworking tools, they may not realize that young children can use them quite handily and should be given the opportunity. But aren't they dangerous, you may wonder? No more dangerous than children's cutting with knives or climbing on climbers when proper safety measures are followed. Set up a woodworking center, post the rules to be followed (Figure 21-1), teach children how to handle each tool, and you will see.

Although wood for the center is easily obtained from carpenters' or contractors' scraps, Sosna (2000) suggests that teachers purchase wood from home centers or lumberyards. Wood from outdoor projects is too often treated with toxic chemicals to combat rot and insects and should not be used. Some is also hardwood which is difficult for children to work with. Pine and poplar are softer and usually inexpensive (p. 38). Even easier for beginners to pound on are tree stumps. Children can cover the tops with nails and that section can then be sliced off for the next round of hammering.

Young children can handle adult tools with little difficulty.

FIGURE 21–1   Safety Rules for Woodworking.

Source: Adapted from "Woodworking: Winning from the beginning" by T. Andrews, 1997, *Texas Child Care, 2*(2); 31.

- Two children in center at a time
- Wear safety goggles at all times
- Use only one tool at a time
- Use hammer, saw, drill only when adult is present
- Return tools to proper place when finished
- Clean up center when finished

Start with basic tools such as two medium or small hammers, screwdrivers, and pliers. More tools can be added as money allows. As children gain more experience in woodworking, you may want to add a workbench to the center. These can be purchased from educational supply companies or made from an old wooden kitchen table with the legs cut down. Other tools you may want to add include: a small steel backsaw, a miter box (saw holder), and an egg-beater-type hand drill. Children can use sandpaper if it is securely fastened around a block of wood. These tools also promote eye-hand coordination and finger-strengthening.

Hang the tools and goggles at children's eye-level from a wall-mounted pegboard on which the tools are outlined and labeled with their names for easy selection and return. Here is more environmental print for children to learn to read. But don't expect the children to create adult-like products. With woodworking as with art, it is the process that is most important for young children, not the product.

ACTIVITIES

1. Introduce a woodworking activity by reading a book to two children.

Read **Building a House.** (Barton, B., 1981, New York: Puffin)

Here is a simple book showing how a house is built. Have the children look at the pictures afterwards and see how many hammerers they can find. Then move over to the woodworking center and show each of the children how to use the hammer. Let them select the small or medium hammer and start pounding nails into the tops of two stumps.

Read **Hammers, Nails, Planks, and Paint.** (Jackson, T. C., 1994, New York: Scholastic)

A multicultural construction crew builds an American house all the way from the architect's drawing to a family moving in. Have the two listeners pick out how many of the crew are doing hammering and what they are hammering. Then let the children select their hammers and start pounding nails into the stumps.

2. Have an alphabet hammering activity. Read **Alphabet Under Construction** (Fleming, D., 2002, New York: Holt) to two children at a time. Have them find which letter the mouse actually hammers: "N." Can they hammer any of the straight-line upper case letters to a board using tongue depressors for the straight lines of the letters? There is a letter poster inside the book that can be hung in the woodworking center. Help them to get started with their own letter N. Then have different children pound together other letters after you read the book to them. Afterwards they can paint their letters. Accept anything they create. Can children make the first letter of their name by pounding large flat-top nails into a stump? Have them try.

REFERENCES

Andrews, T. (1997). Woodworking: Winning from the beginning. *Texas Child Care, 2*(2), 28–33.

Beaty, J. J., & Pratt, L. (2003). *Early literacy in preschool and kindergarten.* Upper Saddle River, NJ: Merrill/Prentice Hall.

Huber, L. K. (1999). Woodworking with young children: You can do it. *Young Children, 54*(6), 32–34.

Leithead, M. (1996). Happy hammering: A hammering activity center with built-in success. *Young Children, 51*(3), 12.

Sosna, D. (2000). More about woodworking with young children. *Young Children, 55*(2), 38–39.

INVENTED SPELLING . . .

CONCEPT

As children see and interact with the environmental print around them in the classroom (e.g., signs, job charts, attendance charts, recipe charts, labels on the aquarium and in each of the learning centers, and dictated stories written down by the teacher), some, but not all of them, will begin to internalize ideas about written words.

Some youngsters will realize, just as they did when they first learned to talk, that everything has a name, and that this name can be written. If you have set up your classroom with a writing center and writing materials, these children may begin experimenting with writing words. These words may be scribbles or letter strings at first. (See EARLY WRITING.) As children become more familiar with letters and their sounds, they may start putting letters together to make words. Not all preschool children will arrive at this point.

Writing their first words should be as exciting as speaking their first words. But some adults are disappointed because the children have not spelled the words correctly. Why should they? Spelling has little to do with children's writing their first words, just as correct pronunciation has little to do with children's speaking their first words. They are trying the best they know how. Proper spelling will come later, not through your corrections, but with experience and refinement.

Instead, some children are putting letters together that sound like the word. First words are often made up mostly of consonants: *skwl* for *school; das* for *days* (Sansome, 1988, p. 14). Literacy specialists call this *invented spelling.* Children are actually *emerging into literacy* right before your eyes. Do not correct them. Encourage them to do all the writing they can. Have them read their words aloud. Challenge them to write a message to a friend, to their parent, to you. Be sure to answer them with your own note. With experience and maturity they will eventually change from invented spelling to conventional spelling on their own—just as they changed from baby talk to conventional speech on their own.

For young children to write words in the first place indicates that they have developed what Opitz (2000, p. 6) calls *phonological awareness* or sound awareness. This awareness comes from hearing words being spoken. But to write words, children must also become aware of certain concepts regarding writing. If children are still writing strings of letters, you will know they have not yet developed this phonological awareness, as defined in Figure 22–1.

Children who use invented spelling have progressed a step beyond this letter-string stage. Their spelling indicates they are phonemically aware, i.e., they know what letters represent the sounds of the words they are writing. They may not be spelling the words conventionally because they do not

FIGURE 22–1 Phonological Awareness.

- written words name things
- written words convey messages that can be read
- words are made up of certain letters
- the letters in the word say the sound of the word
- words represent a sound unit (word awareness)
- words are made up of different parts (syllables)
- words are made up of different sounds (phonemes)

know how yet, but they are exhibiting an exciting breakthrough on the road to emergent literacy. They are spelling words "phonetically." Your job is to support them in this new understanding by providing them with time, writing materials, and opportunities to use their newfound skill. They are experimenting with writing (manipulating the medium) just as they do with any new thing. Having them write on lined paper is not helpful. Young children's experiments with letters and words just do not fit on a line.

What about printing out words correctly for children to copy, you may ask? Then they would not be extracting their own rules about how writing works. You must be careful not to take over the writing process from young children at this point. For emergent writing to occur, children must maintain control of the process themselves (Schrader & Hoffman, 1987, p. 11).

ACTIVITIES

1. Label photos. Have each child in a small group in the writing center choose one of the photos you have put out about classroom activities. Have them paste the photo onto a blank sheet of unlined paper. Talk to each one about the photo and how they would label it ("ETSaBKHS" "It's a block house"). Accept whatever they write, even scribbles.

2. Label children's photos. Put out photos of each child in a small group. Have them paste the photo onto a sheet of paper and have them write: "My name is _____" under the photo ("MI NM S JeremY"). Accept whatever they write.

3. Label paintings. Ask children who are painting at an easel or at a table to write something about their easel picture. Scribbles are acceptable. ("ETS Me N MI DG" "It's me and my dog.") This is known as a "caption picture."

4. Make a list. Children who are beginning to write words enjoy making lists. Have them make a list of foods they like to eat or games they like to play, writing and spelling words as best they can.

REFERENCES

Opitz, M. F. (2000). *Rhymes & reasons: Literature and language play for phonological awareness.* Portsmouth, NH: Heinemann.

Owocki, G. (2001). *Make way for literacy! Teaching the way young children learn.* Portsmouth, NH: Heinemann.

Sansome, R. M. (1988). SKWL DAS: Emerging literacy in children. *Day Care and Early Education, 16*(1), 14–19.

Schrader, C. T., & Hoffman, S. (1987). Encouraging children's early writing efforts. *Day Care and Early Education, 15*(2), 9–13.

Temple, C. A., Nathan, R. C., & Burris, N. A. (1993). *The beginnings of writing.* Boston: Allyn & Bacon.

23 JOURNALING...

CONCEPT

As preschool children begin honing their scribble writing skills along with their drawing ability, teachers need to set up activities that encourage them to practice these skills. Drawing and writing in a journal every day is a favorite method because it combines these abilities in an authentic manner. Children are able to make an actual record of things that happen to them daily. Not only do children get to practice their writing, but the journals they produce give the teacher an overview of their progress.

Journal writing has long been a practice in elementary schools, but journaling with preschool youngsters may be a new experience in many programs. The focus on early literacy now begins in preschool. Young children's writing experiences include notes, messages, signs, lists, letters, and stories that have now become an accepted part of the curriculum.

How can children who do not already write be expected to keep a journal, you may wonder? Children learn to write by writing. They see writing produced around them in the form of environmental print, attendance charts, recipe charts, the daily schedule, lists, and stories the teacher records on newsprint. Now it is their turn to record their own doings. They do not hesitate. Even children who cannot write their own names happily fill their journal pages with scribbles that represent pictures and words (Figure 23–1).

Teachers staple together five sheets of unlined paper, one for every day of the week, and put them into each child's cubby or mailbox on Monday. Staff members work with individuals or small groups of children to get them started, then talk with them daily about their work in positive terms. Some children draw pictures only. Others make lines of scribbles. Some do both. A few write words.

FIGURE 23–1 Four-year-old Urius Traces a Picture of a Puppy, Writes About it, and Signs His Name in His Journal.

ACTIVITIES

1. Read *Diary of a Worm.* (Cronin, D., 2003, New York: Joanna Cotler) This fanciful tale has the date at the top of the page and a simple text under the pictures telling something the worm did that day. For instance, on March 29, the worm tells how he tried to teach spider how to dig. After reading this story to a small group, go back to one of the days and write the date at the top of a newsprint pad. Ask your listeners what they would record for this day if they were the worm. You can record what they tell you. Then give them each a blank page labeled March 29 and have them record whatever they think the worm would write/draw. Help them get started.

2. Read *Zoom! Zoom! Zoom! I'm Off to the Moon!* (Yaccarino, D., 1997, New York: Scholastic Press) Here is another first person story of a little boy who blasts off and goes to the moon. After you reread this story, ask your small group what they think the boy would write/draw in his journal about his trip. Give them blank paper to write/draw what they would write if they were the boy who went to the moon.

3. Take children on a field trip to the zoo. Give them journals to take with them. Take photos or buy picture postcards of the animals. Have them each mount a picture in their journal and write on a page about their trip to the zoo. Or take a pretend trip to the zoo by reading **Going to the Zoo** (Paxton, T., 1996, New York: Morrow) about a boy and girl going with their father to the zoo and seeing elephants, monkeys, a bear, a kangaroo, seals, a lion, and birds. Can they pretend to be the boy or girl and write/draw in their journal about their trip to the zoo? Put out plastic zoo animals and ask each child in your small reading group to choose one and write in her journal what she saw in the zoo.

4. Take a real or pretend trip to the beach or to an aquarium. Buy or use old postcards of a beach or the ocean. Read one of the following books and afterwards give children a chance to paste a postcard on a page and write/draw what they saw on their pretend trip. Scribbles are okay.

- *My Visit to the Aquarium*[*] (Aliki, 1993, New York: HarperCollins)
- *Famous Seaweed Soup*[*] (Martin, A. T., 1993, Morton Grove, IL: Whitman)
- *Beach Feet*[*] (Reiser, L., 1996, New York: Greenwillow)
- *Is This a House for Hermit Crab?* (McDonald, M., 1990, New York: Orchard)
- *Where Does the Trail Lead?*[*] (Albert, B., 1991, New York: Simon & Schuster)

5. Take a picnic to a nearby park or playground. Afterwards, read **Chicken Chickens** (Gorbachev, V., 2001, New York: North-South Books) about two little chicken children who were afraid to go down the slide. What did your children eat? What did your children do on the playground? Have them draw/scribble-write about it in their journals (see Figures 23–2 and 23–3).

FIGURE 23–2 Michael Draws and Asks His Teacher to Write, "Ants Like to Eat My Ham and Cheese Sandwich."

*Multicultural

FIGURE 23–3 Ricci Loved the Picnic and Filled Her Journal Page With This Caption Picture—"I'm a Picnic Full of Sunshine."

6. *Take children on a real or imagined trip to a nearby construction site.* Have them take their journals and write/draw about it. Back in the classroom, read ***B Is for Bulldozer: A Construction ABC*** (Sobel, J., 2003, San Diego: Harcourt). Can they find similar construction equipment in the block center? Have them write/draw about a piece of equipment in their journals.

REFERENCES

Jalongo, M. R. (1992). *Early childhood language arts.* Boston: Allyn & Bacon.

Neuman, S. B., & Roskos, K. A. (1993). *Language and literacy in the early years.* Ft. Worth: Harcourt.

 **LARGE FONT WORDS. . .**

CONCEPT

Most picture books for young children have the text written in the same size print font all the way through. In recent years, however, publishers seem to be aware that emergent readers can begin to recognize important words if they are distinguishable from the rest of the text by being printed in a larger font.

We realize that the youngest children still believe it is the pictures that tell the story, but little by little—through maturity and experience with books—children come to understand that it is really the print on the page that tells the reader what to say. They often see the reader running a finger under the words as she reads them, or even pointing to a certain word. These children may eventually do *finger point* reading themselves by running their own finger under a word as they recite it. This usually means it is a word they have memorized in a familiar story (i.e., emergent reading), rather than a word they have decoded in an unfamiliar story (i.e., conventional reading). Nevertheless, it is an important step on the road to becoming literate.

Young children need more than just seeing adults point to the print on a page for them to become guided by print. As child development specialist Schickedanz (1999) points out: "Children must have some specifically print-related knowledge; otherwise, they continue to use picture-guided reading strategies indefinitely" (p.83). Seeing large font words that describe something in a story illustration is a beginning step. Look for these words in some of the current children's picture books.

ACTIVITIES

1. Read *I Know a Rhino.* (Fuge, C., 2002, New York: Sterling Publishing) This simple rhyming story with its inviting illustrations has a little girl interacting with a whimsical rhino, pig, ape, hippo, dragon, giraffe, bear, and leopard. All of the print is large, but at least two and sometimes three words are printed in larger font. "I know a Rhino. We like to take tea. I have two sugars and Rhino has three."

Run your finger under the words as you read them to the child listeners. Stop when you come to the large font words and say them more emphatically. Next time through the story, pause when you come to a large font word and have the listeners chime in. Children easily memorize these words because this is a *predictable book* in which certain words rhyme. But can they point to the actual word that says "Rhino" or "two" or "three"? Eventually some of them will be able to.

2. Print the names of the animals on index cards. Lay the cards in the block center near the shelf of animals and see who can stand a plastic rhino on the card with its name on it. Mix up the cards and have the children try again.

3. Read *Homemade LOVE.* (Hooks, B., 2002, New York: Hyperion) A little African American girl is loved by her mama and papa in very large font words as mama calls her girlpie and Her Sweet sweet, while daddy calls her honey bun and chocolate Dew Drop. This is truly Homemade Love. She finds out there is no "all the time right" when she does something wrong, but there is forgiveness and no need to be afraid at night.

*Large font words help children make the transition
from picture-guided reading to print-guided reading.*

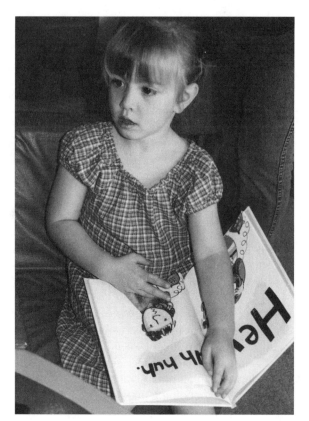

Have your listeners sit close and they will not miss the large font words. What do they think about words so large? Can any of them guess what they say? Reread each page and see if they can.

Print some of the large font words on cards that children in your small reading group can hold. Can anyone match one of the cards to the words in the book? Have them exchange cards and try again as you reread the book.

4. Read other books with special words in large fonts and do the same.

- *Down by the Cool of the Pool* (Mitton, T., 2001, NY: Orchard Books)
- *I Can Do It Too!* (Baicker, K., No date, Brooklyn: Handprint Books)
- *Oonga Boonga* (Wishinsky, F., 1998, New York: Dutton)
- *This Little Chick* (Lawrence, J., 2002, Cambridge, MA: Candlewick)

REFERENCES

Beaty, J. J., & Pratt, L. (2003). *Early literacy in preschool and kindergarten.* Upper Saddle River, NJ: Merrill/Prentice Hall.

Ehri, L. C., & Sweet, J. (1991). Fingerpoint-reading of memorized text: What enables beginners to process the print? *Reading Research Quarterly, 5,* 537–554.

Schickedanz, J. A. (1999). *Much more than the ABCs: The early stages of reading and writing.* Washington, DC: National Association for the Education of Young Children.

Sulzby, R. (1985). Children's emergent reading of favorite storybooks: A developmental study. *Reading Research Quarterly, 20*(4), 458–481.

LEARNING CENTERS . . .

CONCEPT

Learning centers in early childhood classrooms are sectioned-off areas where specific types of activities take place. They are the core of the early childhood curriculum, offering children choices to become involved with Books, Blocks, Dramatic Play, Science, Math, Manipulative Play, Art, Music, Writing, Speaking and Listening, Computers, Woodworking, Cooking, Water Play, and Large Motor Activities. Teachers who focus on early childhood literacy as an important goal make sure that every learning center also contains reading and writing experiences for the children on a daily basis.

ACTIVITIES

1. Entice children to come in. Be creative with your learning centers. Pretend each one is a store that needs to advertise its wares and entice children to come in and explore its offerings. For instance, let the Book Center be a model for other centers. Make this learning center large enough for at least six children at once. You will be reading to small groups of this size. Use colors and designs to attract the youngsters: bright colors of red, yellow, orange, and purple; fluorescent colors of pink and magenta; sparkling colors of silver and gold. Designs can include stars and planets; animal cutouts; seasonal items such as colored leaves for fall, pumpkins and black cats for Halloween; and candles and wreaths for the Christmas and Hanukkah season. Be sure to put out books related to your decorations.

2. Fill the center with appropriate furnishings. Book shelves holding 20 or more books with covers facing out can also be used as room dividers. An overstuffed couch with fluffy pillows, a beanbag chair or two, floor pillows on a soft carpet and, if there is room, an adult rocking chair in the corner can make the center a comfortable and inviting place. Some teachers include an end table with a cassette player, headset, and book tapes.

3. Advertise the books you are featuring. You should advertise the books you are featuring for each month with book jackets, signs, posters, balloons, or other special attractions that you make or purchase. What about having an alphabet tree in the corner for **Chicka Chicka Boom Boom** (Martin, B., & Archambault, J., 1989, New York: Simon & Schuster) when you feature alphabet books? Or you might feature the books of Ezra Jack Keats for one month with a banner from Demco, Inc. (1-800-356-1200) mounted on the wall or hung from a clothesline against the wall, saying "Read About Peter's Neighborhood." Put out your Keats books: **The Snowy Day, Whistle for Willie, Peter's Chair, A Letter to Amy,** and **Pet Show.** Purchase the Peter character doll and Willie dog for the children to use in their pretending, or make your own characters from cutouts. (See CHARACTER DOLLS, CUTOUTS.)

4. Promote reading of the books. Put up a chart with the names of the books listed and a blank line with space enough for sticking on a peel-off star every time a child reads one of the books. How will you know which children looked at which book? Record their names when they come to you to get their stars. Children will then have to figure out the name of the book on your chart in order to stick on their star in the right place. Some will already know how to compare the book in their hand with the name on the chart. Can a child read the same book more than once? Of course! That's the point of it: bringing books and children together—again and again.

Hang this book in the dramatic play center.

Call for the "Demco Library and Reading Promotions" catalog (1-800-356-1200) for an idea of the book promotional materials available. If your budget is tight, make your own. Wall hangings include: ***Whistle for Willie, The Snowy Day,*** "Books are Big Fun" (shows a dinosaur), ***Strega Nona,*** and "Hug a Book." Posters and banners include: "Dive into Reading," "Be a Reader," and "Books Are Friends Forever." Book marks, pencils, and buttons are also available.

5. Play games with books. Play games with books. Fasten a long string to a book with a card at the other end of the string printed with its title. Then hide the book in one of the other centers with its card dangling out for anyone to see. Whoever spots this card must first read the title before they can unearth the book from its hiding place. Can the children do it without help?

6. Hang a book in every learning center. Books should not be restricted to the Book Center alone. Each learning center should feature a book-of-the-month as a lead-in to the topic being pursued. Fasten a long string to the wall in each center with a kitchen clip dangling at the other end. Clip the book-of-the-month to the kitchen clips in the various centers. Children must unfasten the book from the clip to read it. (Good for finger strengthening.) When children see each book, they will want one of the adult staff members to read it. Great! Just what you hoped would happen as a lead-in to the planned activity. Gather a small group in the center and read the book.

In the Block Center, hang the book ***B Is for Bulldozer, A Construction ABC*** (Sobel, J., 2003, San Diego: Harcourt) if you have gone on a field trip to a construction site. Provide a box of props for their block building activities with string for wires, sticks, stones, little trucks, construction vehicles, and block people. Also include plastic hard hats for the children builders.

In the Dramatic Play Center, hang the book ***Cleversticks*** (Ashley, B., 1991, New York: Crown) if you are featuring an Asian restaurant or preparing rice in the Cooking Center. Have several pairs of chopsticks available for practice in picking up small items.

In the Science Center, hang ***Carlos and the Squash Plant*** (Stevens, J. R., 1993, Flagstaff, AZ: Northland) or ***Flower Garden*** (Bunting, E., 1994, San Diego: Harcourt) if you have put out seeds, potting soil, paper cups, and a trowel as preparation for a planting activity.

———

*Multicultural

A bead-stringing experience in the Manipulative/Math Center calls for a book like **A String of Beads**[*] (Reid, M. S., 1997, New York: Dutton). Counting/sorting activities call for books such as **Cat Count** (Lewin, B., 2003, New York: Henry Holt) or **Counting Crocodiles** (Sierra, J., 1997, San Diego: Harcourt). Put up a chart on the wall for children to indicate the number of plastic animal counters they have sorted out for each species. Have another chart with children's names and a peel-off sticker showing a pet they own or hope to own.

7. Decorate each of the learning centers. Posters, charts, graphs, banners, photos, and wall hangings can decorate each of the learning centers, making your classroom an exciting place to be. Children's art can be mounted on colored construction paper, wallpaper, colored burlap, calico, silk, or satin in a rainbow of colors to brighten every center. Let children choose their own backing and help them mount their pictures. As Taylor (2002) notes:

Color has been found to influence academic achievement. For example, red is a good choice for areas planned for gross motor activities and concept development activities; yellow is good for music and art activities; and green, blue, and purple are effective in reading areas. (p. 369)

REFERENCES

Fye, M. A. S., & Mumpower, J. P. (2001). Lost in space? Design learning areas for today. *Dimensions of Early Childhood, 29*(2), 16–22.

Seefeldt, C. (2002). *Creating rooms of wonder.* Beltsville, MD: Gryphon House.

Sloane, M. W. (2000). Make the most of learning centers. *Dimensions of Early Childhood, 28*(1), 16–20.

Taylor, B. J. (2002). *Early childhood program management: People and procedures* (4th ed.). Upper Saddle River, NJ: Merrill/Prentice Hall.

Warner, L. (2003). Planning effective classroom discovery centers. *Dimensions of Early Childhood, 31*(1), 22–27.

---

[*]Multicultural

 LISTENING . . .

CONCEPT

Children learn to speak by hearing words spoken around them, just as they learn to read in part by hearing stories read to them. But to hear these words and stories, children need to listen. Jalongo (1996) tells us: "Listening is the process used to convert spoken language and sound into meaning in the mind" (p. 21). Young children need to learn to listen to the speaking going on around them. How do they do it? First, they need to be able to hear clearly. If they pay little attention to what you are saying to them or do not seem to hear what you say, they may need to be screened for hearing impairments or attention deficits. Do not wait until they enter elementary school. The earlier such deficits can be identified, the sooner they can be corrected.

Second, children need to be able to hear words being spoken. Every early childhood classroom is full of talking and the noise of boisterous children at work and play. Still, you should be able to hear one another talking without raising your voice. If you hear only loud noises and shouting or if you spend too much time trying to quiet the children, you may need to sound-proof the room.

Create a Physical Listening Environment

To be able to listen to and hear what you are saying, children need to filter out other extraneous sounds, noises, and distractions around them. Look at the classroom itself to see what can be done to cut down the noise. It can be converted into an enjoyable physical listening environment in a number of ways (Figure 26–1) without seriously disrupting children in their normal activities.

ACTIVITIES

1. Start with the ceiling. What do you see when you look up? Is the ceiling smooth and flat? You may need to recommend that acoustical ceiling tiles be installed. Hanging cloth mobiles from the ceiling also helps.

2. Next, look at walls and windows. Various types of wall coverings can be used to absorb noise. Curtains or drapes at windows absorb more noise than blinds or shutters. Corkboards for bulletin

FIGURE 26–1 Physical Listening Environment.

- Use acoustical ceiling tiles
- Hang cloth mobiles from ceiling
- Use curtains or drapes at windows
- Use cork panels and bulletin boards
- Use colored burlap on room dividers
- Use fabric-wrapped fiberboard on walls
- Have fluffy area rugs on carpeting
- Use floor pillows, cloth bean bag chairs
- Place thick towels under pounding stumps
- Have cloth dolls, puppets, stuffed animals

boards and cork panels in learning centers are excellent sound absorbers. Colored burlap can be fastened to backs of room dividers or used for wall hangings. Any kind of cloth material absorbs sound. Fabric-wrapped fiberboard can cover an entire wall.

3. What about floor coverings? Placing fluffy area rugs here and there on the carpeting provides sound absorption. Floor pillows, cloth bean-bag chairs, and floor rockers also help. Programs without funds for expensive materials can cut apart large cardboard cartons or delivery cases, cover them with burlap, hang them with colorful bath towels, and use them for room dividers. Place a thick towel under pounding stumps in the woodworking center. Think "cloth" when ordering materials: cloth dolls, book characters, and puppets; stuffed animals, pillows, and dress-up clothes. What else can be covered with absorbent material?

CONCEPT

Teach Children to Become Active Listeners

Children can be taught to listen. Active listeners become quiet when someone speaks to them. They listen for key words. They wait until the speaker is finished before responding. You can help children become active listeners by talking to each individual in the class every day, using your own active listening skills. Keep a list of the children's names handy and check them off each time you speak to an individual. If you miss anyone, be sure to speak to them the next day. What kinds of things might you talk about?

1. Greet each child in the morning, using their names and saying something about their trip to school. Give them a chance to answer.

2. Talk to a child on one of the toy phones when you see him near a second phone. Say, "Pick up the phone, Jeremy. Someone wants to talk to you."

3. Talk to a child in one of the learning centers. Say, "Oh, Lily, the colors you are using in your painting are just like the ones in your shirt." Or "Andy, what an interesting building you're making with the unit blocks."

4. Talk to the child next to you at lunch. Say, "I'm glad we're having applesauce today. Apples are my favorite fruit. What about you?"

5. Talk to a child in conflict with another child. Say, "How do you think he feels, Ramon? Look at his face. What does it tell you?"

Children 3 to 5 years old may not understand everything you say. Kratcoski and Katz (1998) suggest the following teacher communication behaviors to help children understand:

- Use simple sentences.
- Speak slowly and clearly.
- Vary your tone/expression to emphasize key words.
- Pause between sentences.
- Try to comment more than question. (p. 31)

Children can also learn to listen from simple listening games. Include at least one specific listening activity every week for a small group of children in one of the classroom learning centers.

ACTIVITIES

1. Book Center. Read and talk about one of the following books with a listening theme:

Mice Squeak, We Speak (dePaola, T., 1997, New York: Putnam)

Polar Bear, Polar Bear, What Do You Hear?* (Martin, B., & Carle, E., 1991, New York: Henry Holt)

Children listen to tape and follow movement directions.

The Sound of Day, The Sound of Night (O'Neill, M., 2003, New York: Farrar, Straus, & Giroux)

Listen to the Desert (Mora, P., 1994, New York: Clarion)

2. Block Center. Play a "Who Is Missing?" game. Take out five farm animals (cow, sheep, goat, horse, pig) and say the name of each animal. Put all of them in a box. Now, say "Oh-oh, one of the animals is missing. I wonder which one." Take out four of the animals and have children say names and guess. Play this several times with different animals missing. Then say: "Okay, now build a barn or a corral for these animals so they won't run away." (This game can also be played with jungle animals, zoo animals, or block people.)

3. Art Center. Make animal headbands with ears for each of the animals in the book **Polar Bear, Polar Bear, What Do You Hear?** (polar bear, lion, hippopotamus, flamingo, zebra, boa constrictor, elephant, leopard, peacock, walrus). Children can color the bands like the book animal colors. You can help with the ears. Children can wear the headband of their animal and make its noise as you read. They will need to listen closely so that they hear the words and come in at the right time.

4. Music Center. Put on a music tape or CD that asks children to listen and follow directions. *Kids in Motion* leads children through the "Tummy Tango" and "Beanbag Boogie." *Where Is Thumbkin?* has children wiggle fingers, touch toes, and act like an elephant. *Wiggle Wiggle* has children shake, jump, and wiggle. (All are available from Lakeshore 1-800-778-4456.)

5. At Circle Time. Play "Gotcha!" Tell the children to listen carefully to what each animal says and if they think the animal is wrong or trying to fool them, say "Gotcha!" Then you pretend to be each of the animals, making a correct sound for all but one:

"The dog says *ruff-ruff!*"

"The cat says *meow!*"

"The mouse says *squeak-squeak!*"

"The horse says *meow!*"

---

*Multicultural

Use as many animals as you want, or play a variant of this game with sounds of motor vehicles, musical instruments, people walking, or anything else you can think of that makes a special sound. Play a different sound-listening game like this every day to help children concentrate on listening.

REFERENCES

Beaty, J. J. (2004). *Skills for preschool teachers* (7th ed.). Upper Saddle River, NJ: Merrill/Prentice Hall.

Jalongo, M. R. (1996). Teaching children to become better listeners. *Young Children, 51*(2), 21–26.

Klenck, L. (2001). Playing with literacy in preschool classrooms. *Childhood Education, 77*(3), 150–157.

Kratcoski, A. M., & Katz, K. B. (1998). Conversing with young language learners in the classroom. *Young Children, 53*(3), 30–33.

LITERACY BAGS. . .

CONCEPT

Literacy bags, sometimes called "bookbags," "book packs," or "book backpacks," are containers holding paperback books along with book extension props and activities such as puppets, character cutouts, a book audiotape, and an activities sheet for parents. Literacy bags are intended for home use. It is important that parents become aware of their children's literacy activities in school and give support and encouragement at home.

When you talk to parents, explain to them the benefits of reading aloud to children, invite them to watch and participate in classroom read-aloud activities, and finally tell them their children will be bringing home literacy bags with books for them to read to their children. You can develop your own lending library of paperback copies of the same books you are reading in the classroom along with various tapes or props. Children can sign out the literacy bags for week-long use. This gives parents enough time to listen to the tape, read the story aloud, talk about the book, and play the activities with their children. According to Meier (2000), advantages for using literacy bags in the home include:

- Helps children develop a strong sense of self and independence in school literacy.
- Recognizes the respect that parents afford teachers.
- Coordinates preschool literacy learning with kindergarten goals and practices.
- Recognizes and builds on the literacy of entire families.
- Shows the variety of child-created literacy practices invented in children's home. (p.133)

Meier notes what one parent thought about the bookbag program: "I like the bookbag program because it gave the kids a sense of independence, and Akilah felt proud to have her own book come home. She took care of it, and she wanted to read it as soon as she got home. She wanted to read *her* book" (p. 133).

Second-language speakers may want to listen to the tape first while looking at book pages. Parents who are not used to reading to their children may want to listen to the tape to gain confidence in their own reading aloud. Neuman (1997) feels that engaging parents and children in mutual activities that include book reading, but are not limited to it, may constitute the richest potential for supporting children's early literacy development (p. 119).

Most parents want to support their children's literacy development but may not know how. The activities sheet that you include in the bookbag can give them suggestions of how to read the story, what questions to ask the children about the story, how to get the children involved in the story reading, and what extension activities they can do. Book pack programs from Scholastic (1-800-724-6527) for under $10 contain a book, an audiocassette of the book, and an activities sheet. Scholastic's cultural character book pack program includes the books shown in Figure 27–1.

ACTIVITIES

1. Make your own literacy bags. Make the packs from large baggies from the supermarket, or backpacks can be purchased from discount stores. See-through take-home backpacks and tote bags can also be purchased from Lakeshore Learning Materials (1-800-421-5354). Childcraft Educational Corporation (1-800-219-5253) also features "book buddy bags." If a tape cassette of your book is not

Abiyoyo (African)	*Mama Do You Love Me?* (Alaskan)
Aunt Flossie's Hats (African American)	*Silly Sally* (English)
Bringing the Rain to Kapiti Plain (African)	*Strega Nona* (Italian)
Corduroy (African American)	*Ten, Nine, Eight* (African American)
Dancing with the Indians (Afr. American & Indian)	*Tikki Tikki Tembo* (Chinese)
Families are Different (Korean and Anglo American)	*Ty's One Man Band* (African American)
Jamaica's Find (Afr. American & Anglo American)	*What Mary Jo Shared* (Afr. American)

FIGURE 27–1 Book Packs from Scholastic.

Flower Garden (African American)	*Snowy Day* (African American)
Lion Dancer (Chinese)	*Song and Dance Man* (Anglo)
Mama, Do You Love Me? (Native Alaskan)	*Three Little Javelinas* (Hispanic)
Saturday Night at the Dinosaur Stomp	

FIGURE 27–2 Books and Tapes from Scholastic.

available, make your own. (See BOOK TAPES.) Scholastic (1-800-724-6527) offers the paperback books listed in Figure 27–2 with audiocassettes for under $8.00.

Include in each literacy bag (in addition to book and tape) cutouts of the characters made from color page copies from the books, a puzzle made from a color page copy from the book, two or three crayons and blank paper, and an activities sheet. Find out which families do not have cassette players and have little hand-held sets available for borrowing.

2. Make an activity sheet for *Mama, Do You Love Me?* (Joose, B. M., 1991, San Francisco: Chronicle Books)

First, read the book to the child who will be sitting on your lap or close to you. Read it again if the child agrees.

As you re-read the story, get the child involved by asking questions.

On the title page, you could ask: Do you think the little girl loves her mama? How can you tell?

Turn the page and ask: Do you think the mama loves her little girl? How can you tell?

On the next page, you might ask the child to find the raven's treasure, the dog's tail, and the whale's spout.

On the next page, have the child point to the "umiak," the "puffin," and so on through the book.

Play the book tape with the child looking at each page. Help the child turn the page when she hears the signal.

The child can play with the cutout characters (mama, girl, raven, whale, puffin, walrus, and polar bear); she can also trace them and color them. Or include a character doll.

Now ask the child to read the story to you. She may tell you that she can't read, but you can have her read the pictures in the book. (Most children delight in "reading" to their parents. This book should already be familiar to children since they have read it in the classroom, as well.)

Check off which of these activities you did with the child. Write which ones the child especially liked and any other comments you want to make. Read the story several times to the child, asking questions about what's happening in the story, playing the tape of the story, and asking the child to "read" the story to you.

Include a character doll in the literacy bag.

3. Make an activity sheet for *Saturday Night at the Dinosaur Stomp.* (Shields, C. D., 1999, Cambridge, MA: Candlewick Press)

Have the children do the "dinosaur stomp" as shown by the foot directions on the inside cover. Play the music from the tape included.

Help the child make dinosaur footprints like those in the book. Place them in a trail through the house for everyone to follow.

Use the dinosaur cutouts included and have the child match them with the dinosaur pictures in the book.

Play with the little plastic dinosaurs from the classroom that are included in this literacy bag.

REFERENCES

Barbour, A. C. (1998/99). Home literacy bags: Promote family involvement. *Childhood Education, 75*(2), 71–75.

Beaty, J. J., & Pratt, L. (2003). *Early literacy in preschool and kindergarten.* Upper Saddle River, NJ: Merrill/Prentice Hall.

Dever, M. T., & Burts, D. C. (2002). Using family literacy bags to enhance family involvement. *Dimensions of Early Childhood, 30*(1), 16–20.

Meier, D. R. (2000). *Scribble scrabble: Learning to read and write.* New York: Teachers College Press.

Neuman, S. B. (1997). Guiding young children's participation in early literacy development: A family literacy program for adolescent mothers. *Early Child Development and Care, 127–128,* 119–129.

MESSAGES . . .

CONCEPT

Writing a simple message to someone else is an authentic writing experience many preschool children enjoy—especially because it is such a grownup thing to do. Teachers who are aware of their children's writing skills often set up situations in which children have opportunities to write messages to other children telling them something that has happened, asking them a question, making a comment on something they did, or inviting them to do something or go somewhere. Whether or not the children can write is not the point. The message can be done in scribble writing or drawing.

One way to introduce children to message writing is to start with a daily message sheet that you write for the whole class that asks for a response from the children as they arrive each day. It can be written on a large piece of unlined paper or newsprint clipped to a board or easel at children's eye level. Paper is better than a write-and-wipe board since the message and responses can be preserved for review of the children's writing progress. Write the day and date at the top, and then your message. Save plenty of room for replies.

What if the youngsters do not know how to write a response? This may be the case with most of your children. Put out marking pens of different colors and encourage them to respond in scribble writing or drawing in any way they want. Even a dot is acceptable! Have them sign their names or initials after their response if they can. If they ask you for help, give them your support but have them try to scribble, print, or draw their comments on their own.

Make the daily message a simple one based on a common experience which you read to the children and invite those who want to write a response. For instance, you could write: **I rode to school this morning on my bike. It was fun.** Children can then scribble or draw their replies. Some may write a real word or two. Others may draw a bus or car or a person.

Be careful not to correct spelling or grammar in the children's responses. You want them to feel good about real writing and to continue with their efforts. Not everyone may be willing to try at first, but when they see what the others are doing and how enjoyable it is for them, they may eventually join in.

As children become more adept at writing messages, have them think about writing a message to someone who is not present. You may need to work with individuals as they write messages to others, asking them to think about the other person who will receive it. When children are just beginning to write, they are often preoccupied with just getting anything down. They may not have thought about the other person at all. You may need to point out that their response is not for themselves but for the other person.

ACTIVITIES

1. Make message journals. Just as you made daily journals for the children to write in, change this to a "message journal" for individuals after the total group has had practice responding to your daily messages. Staple together and date five sheets of paper with the title "Message Journal" on the front. Then each morning one of the staff members can write a brief message at the top of a dated page for each child. Make it personal. For example: "Your new sneakers are cool." or "I like what you built in the block center." You can read your message for each child, and have them "write" or draw a response which they in turn read to you.

Children can write an invitation to their mothers.

2. Read *A Letter to Amy** (Keats, E. J., 1984, New York: HarperCollins) or *Welcome to Kindergarten* (Rockwell, A., 2001, New York: Walker & Co.). Sometimes a message is an invitation. In *A Letter to Amy,* Peter invites Amy to his birthday party. But he forgets to include all the important information. His mother points out that he didn't tell Amy when to come. So Peter writes "It is this Saturday at 2" on the back of the sealed envelope. In *Welcome to Kindergarten,* the kindergarten teacher invites Tim to visit kindergarten where he will be going next year.

Have the children write an invitation to their mothers to visit the class on Mother's Day.

3. Read *We Are Best Friends* (Aliki, 1982, New York: Mulberry) or *Jenny's Journey** (Samton, S.W., 1991, New York: Viking). Sometimes messages are letters to friends. Both of these books tell the story about a friend who moves away. In one, the friend who is left behind writes to the friend who moves away. In the other, it is the friend who moves away who writes the first letter. Read the story several times. Then have the children choose parts and reenact the story, including the letter writing. (See STORY REENACTMENTS.)

4. Read *Good Morning Franny, Good Night Franny.* (Hearn, E., 1984, Toronto: The Women's Educational Press) In this story, Franny, a city girl in a wheelchair, becomes friends with Ting, a Chinese girl, and plays with her every day in the park. She teaches Ting some words in English, which Ting writes in her notebook. One day Franny finds that Ting has moved away. She is sad until she finds the surprise message that Ting has left her. On the sidewalk at the entrance to the park is written "Good morning Franny." On the sidewalk at the exit she wrote "Good night Franny." Bring out the sidewalk chalk and have a small group at a time write messages on the walk outside the building.

REFERENCES

Beaty, J. J., & Pratt, L. (2003). *Early literacy in preschool and kindergarten.* Upper Saddle River, NJ: Merrill/Prentice Hall.

Hall, N. (2000). Interactive writing with young children, *Childhood Education, 76*(60), 358–364.

Schickedanz, J. A. (1999). *Much more than the ABCs: The early stages of reading and writing.* Washington, DC: National Association for the Education of Young Children.

NAMES . . .

CONCEPT

Children's names have long been an important part of early childhood learning and teaching. Not only do they identify the children for the teaching staff and their classmates, but they also identify the children for themselves. Children who enter the program at age three may still have a rather shaky image of who they are. Suddenly they hear their name called, not once but many times, by the teachers and their classmates. When they hear their name they respond to it. This is who they are: Allison, Jennifer, Kaitlyn, Megan, Melissa, Shandra, or Yolanda; Brandon, Dylan, Jesse, Keshawn, Kyle, Miguel, Travis, or Tyrone. People ask them what their names are and they tell them with confidence.

Children also like to hear their names sung in greeting songs, good-bye songs, getting-ready songs, and pick-up songs to familiar tunes such as *Lazy Mary:*

> Keshawn Williams will you pick up,
>
> Will you pick up, will you pick up,
>
> Keshawn Williams will you pick up,
>
> The blocks and trucks today.

Then they begin seeing their names written on name tags, place mats, circle time mats, cubbies, crayon boxes, art work, toothbrushes, blankets, and computer printouts. Soon they recognize that those printed symbols are also who they are. Names seem to be their personal property. Those written names identify things that belong to them.

Using only uppercase letters is best at first. Children do seem to find it easier to write uppercase letters. However, the print they see in books contains both upper- and lowercase letters. Exposure to both kinds of print helps them become accustomed to both.

Next the teachers want them to write their own names on art work, writing paper, and sign-up sheets. Some children have already learned at home how to write their names. But many newcomers have not. If you have a mixed-age class, the five's may have had more experience with names than the three's. But now everyone is encouraged to print their names, at least the first letter.

Learning to Write Their Names

Teachers may help at first. In years past, teachers often printed out children's names in upper- and lowercase and had them trace them over and over with a marker or their finger. Today some teachers give each child a card with his name printed in large letters for him to copy onto another paper. At first children try to copy and later generate their names on their own, as Genny did in Figure 29–1. Some generate without copying. Some just scribble at first. But many children seem to trace spontaneously without being instructed and then copy their names.

Children have heard their names pronounced aloud. Now they are learning that their names can be written down. They must be words—like the words on the labels for objects in the classroom. Children learn to print the letters in their names even before they know the names of the letters. At first they may omit a letter or scatter the letters around on the paper, sometimes backwards or upside down.

FIGURE 29–1 Four-Year-Old
Genny Scribbles Her Name.

FIGURE 29–2 Steps Toward
Children Writing Their First
Names.

- Children recognize their spoken names
- Children recognize their written names
- Children experiment scribbling their names
- Children trace, copy, or generate letters of their names
- Children print names in proper order
- Children select their name card by first letter alone
- Children learn names of letters in their names
- Children use letters in their names to find and write other words

Although it may take awhile, finally they get it right, usually in the steps shown in Figure 29–2. They then have a repertory of known letters, letters that can be used to write other words.

In the beginning, only the first letter of their name may be familiar. When teachers put out the name cards of everyone in the class and ask children to find theirs, Megan may pick up Melissa's card because she recognizes only the first letter. Remembering that young children start with the general and then learn the specific, you could have Megan compare her name card with Melissa's, having her note that Melissa's name starts with the same letter as hers but Melissa's name is longer. Children eventually memorize the names of the letters in their names and how to write them. Now they are ready to use these same letters for recognizing and writing other words.

ACTIVITIES

1. Play games to help children recognize letters by their names. Have a variety of solid letters such as wood, plastic, magnetic, and cardboard letter sets to be used in matching games and alphabet dominoes.

Have each child become a letter they know and go around the room finding objects (labeled or not) that begin with their letter.

Play a follow-the-directions game in which you have children holding a letter card sit in chairs in a circle while you call out directions: "b's wiggle both your feet," or "h's shake hands with a's," or "j's jump up and down" or "c's clap your hands."

2. *Read books with name words.* Read ***Z Goes Home.*** (Agee, J., 2003, New York: Hyperion)

> The large capital letter Z hops down from the Zoo page and starts on his way home passing other uppercase letters representing all sorts of objects, one to a page: A is an alien; B is a bridge; C is an angelfood cake that Z eats a piece of. He even gets caught in an Earthquake. Can your listeners see the "E"? What about "F" as a Factory? Read this book to no more than two at a time. Have them help you discover the letters. Next time through, see if they can tell what object each letter names.

> Read ***A, My Name is Alice.*** (Bayer, J., 1984, New York: Puffin)

> After you have read this classic jump-rope-rhyme book all the way through to a small group, see if any of your listeners can play the game using their own names. "A my name is Alice, and my husband's name is Alex; We come from Alaska, and we sell ants."

> Read ***Eleanor, Ellatony, Ellencake, and Me.*** (Rubin, C. M., 2003, Columbus, OH: McGraw Hill Children's Publishing)

> In this humorous rhyming story Eleanor starts out with one name, but then each member of her family calls her something different: Elle, Nana's precious belle; Punch, Grandpa's playmate; Eleanora, Dad's movie star; Ellatony, Mom's little elbow macaroni. Finally she rebels and decides that she will be Ellie and nothing else, and so she is.

> Show the children how you can change Ellie's name with magnetic letters. Start with Eleanor and then go through the different changes in the story. Can your listeners tell which is which? Have one listener at a time try writing her own name in magnetic letters. Children are often sensitive about their names or nicknames, so tread carefully about changing theirs even in fun.

REFERENCES

Beaty, J. J., & Pratt, L. (2003). *Early literacy in preschool and kindergarten.* Upper Saddle River, NJ: Merrill/Prentice Hall.

Schickedanz, J. A. (1999). *Much more than the ABCs.* Washington, DC: National Association for the Education of Young Children.

Temple, C.A., Nathan, R. G., & Burris, N. A. (1993). *The beginnings of writing.* Boston: Allyn & Bacon.

PHOTOS . . .

CONCEPT

Cameras in the preschool classroom? Yes. Photos have several important roles to play in children's early literacy development, as demonstrated in Figure 30–1. Because young children feel that it is pictures rather than text that tell the story in picture books, photos can be valuable storytellers, as well as helping children make the transition from picture-governed to print-governed reading. Photos can also stimulate children's telling and writing their own stories. In addition, personal photos promote children's self-image, showing the youngsters what they look like as well as showing off their block structures, art products, and science projects for all to see. For teachers, photos of children's work can provide a pictorial record of their achievements useful for individual assessment and for children's portfolios. Outside of the classroom, photos extend children's school learning into their homes as children take home photos of their accomplishments.

Kinds of Cameras

Almost any kind of camera is useful for the taking of pictures, but each kind has its own advantages. Digital cameras make traditional photo developing unnecessary. The photos produced are immediately accessible for teachers and children. Once entered into the computer they can be enlarged, reduced, cropped, and printed off for numerous classroom applications. Instant cameras such as Polaroids also produce photos for immediate use. The sooner children can see a photo of the intricate block structure they just built, the easier it is for them to record their story about it on paper or a tape. In their excellent book, *Picture This,* Entz and Galarza (2000) tell us: "Digital and instant photography helps young children to revisit their first-hand experiences shortly after they occur and to fix them in time. Pictures stimulate the recall of direct experiences and the use of words as memory triggers to recall these concrete events" (p. xi).

On the other hand, programs without digital or instant cameras can find other means for making photos quickly available. Film from regular 35mm cameras can be developed rapidly through one-hour-processing outlets found in copy stores, discount stores, supermarkets, drugstores, and camera stores. These photos can then be enlarged or reduced and duplicated on color copiers. A computer with a scanner can perform these same tasks and then print off the photos on a color printer.

FIGURE 30–1 Using Photography to Promote Early Literacy.

- Stimulates use of words to describe photos, tell stories
- Stimulates recall of direct experiences
- Promotes conversation and new vocabulary
- Stimulates children's interest in classroom activities
- Helps children make own books and make up stories
- Helps children make and read photo labels of toys
- Extends school learning into the home
- Promotes child's self-image

Young children can be involved in taking pictures on their own.

Young children can also be involved in taking their own pictures using simple point-and-click, disposable cameras without fear of their breaking an expensive camera.

ACTIVITIES

1. Use photos to promote making books and telling stories.

Whenever the class goes on a field trip, take a camera along to record what they see and do. Back in the classroom, use the photos to engage the children in telling a story about their field trip. Some teachers make books with a photo on each page accompanied by the children's words printed in large font print. Children love to read over and over their own books of *Our Visit to the Fire Station* or *Our Trip to the Library.*

Take photos of favorite book character dolls eating pretend food, sleeping in doll beds, or riding in toy trucks and have children make up an adventure story about the characters to be dictated to the teacher and made into an illustrated book.

2. Take photos of the steps to build, make, or create something.
  - Use a recipe, ingredients, and utensils to cook something
  - Build a block building from start to finish
  - Do a science experiment on objects that sink or float

3. Take photos of individual children to be used in classroom activities.

Mount a small photo of each child on an attendance card, along with the child's name, to be hooked onto an attendance board daily by the child when he is in attendance.

Laminate (or use clear contact paper) photo and the name of each child onto a playing card. Make two similar decks of cards for use in sorting, matching, lotto, and who-is-missing? games.

Make a photo puzzle of each child by laminating large photos (5 × 7 or 8 × 10) on squares of cardboard and cutting them into pieces.

4. Read book about children taking photos, then make up own stories.

Read ***Pascual's Magic Pictures*** (Gage, A., 1996, Minneapolis, MN: Carolrhoda) about the Guatemalan boy Pascual who wants a disposable camera like the ones the tourists have. He saves the money he makes selling tourist trinkets, buys the camera, and hurries off to the jungle to take pictures of the howler monkeys. But he is frightened by their tremendous howls, drops the camera, and doesn't find it till the next day, all used up. The monkeys have taken wonderful closeup pictures of themselves and one of Pascual down below!

Have children use disposable cameras to take pictures for stories of their own which they dictate to you for making their own books.

REFERENCES

Beaty, J. J., & Pratt, L. (2003). *Early literacy for preschool and kindergarten.* Upper Saddle River, NJ: Merrill/Prentice Hall.

Entz, S., & Galarza, S. L. (2000). *Picture this: Digital and instant photography activities for early childhood learning.* Thousand Oaks, CA: Corwin Press.

PICTURES, CAPTION. . .

CONCEPT

Children's first story writing often takes the form of pictures that they draw or paint about something they have done or something that has happened to them. The story may be one initiated by the teacher who suggests they draw a picture of a field trip they have taken or a science project they have worked on. On the other hand, it may originate with a child who wants to draw a picture in her journal of something that happened to her. When children ask the teacher to write their story on their picture, usually at the top or bottom, we call these drawings *caption pictures*. As children become more experienced drawing caption pictures, creating stories for them, and hearing the stories read aloud, some will be able to collaborate with the teacher and begin to write their own captions.

What can children learn from their caption pictures? Teachers who involve children in this kind of drawing say that caption pictures help children to:

- make a connection between spoken and written language
- see how their spoken language is written down
- see what words look like that are used to label objects in their pictures
- see how the words they spoke are spelled
- see how a story is written
- develop a "sense of story"
- begin to write their own captions/stories

ACTIVITIES

1. Read *I Will Never Not Ever Eat a Tomato.* (Child, L., 2000, Cambridge, MA: Candlewick) One teacher tells how it quickly became one of the children's favorites. They loved to act out the story with different children taking the roles of Charlie, the tricky brother, and Lola, the fussy-eating sister. The actors often made up their own lines about why they would not eat peas, carrots, potatoes, spaghetti, bananas, apples, cheese, fish sticks, and especially tomatoes.

The teacher invited these 4- and 5-year-olds to make their own book, only this time about their favorite foods and why they liked to eat them. All of the children who drew pictures dictated picture captions to the teacher who wrote them down. The results were somewhat different from what the teacher expected. While many of the children focused on themselves alone as the teacher had expected, some followed the lead of the tomato book and included brothers and sisters. (See Figures 31–1 and 31–2.)

From this experience, the teacher learned that:

- Food made an excellent topic for children to draw and write about.
- Using a favorite book as a lead-in to drawing and writing activities was especially successful.
- Listening to children's picture captions and following their lead could result in valuable new literacy experiences.
- Starting with one particular picture could lead to the creation of an entire book with a plot and characters.
- Caption pictures can help teachers discover which children have developed a "sense of story."

FIGURE 31–1 "Me and My Brother Eat Cottage Cheese, Milk, Dressing, Chicken, Bananas, and Hot Peppers."

FIGURE 31–2 "My Sisters and I Are Eating Pizza While Mom Is Walking In the Door."

2. Start with a picture. In this case, the teacher decided to start with the picture that most resembled an on-going story: Figure 31–2 ("My sisters and I are eating pizza while mom is walking in the door."). She asked the child artist if she wanted to make a whole book. The girl agreed. The teacher asked the girl: "What happens next?"

> Girl: *"Mom is mad because we started before she came in."*
>
> Teacher: *"What does she do? Can you draw a picture about that?"*

Once the girl had drawn the picture and dictated the caption, the teacher continued, asking her, "And then what happens?"

Once the story was completed, the teacher wrote captions on the pictures, just as the girl dictated them, and stapled the book together along with a cover the girl made. The book was placed in the book center for everyone to read.

FIGURE 31–3   "I'm Happy When I Eat Spaghetti and My Spaghetti Is Happy Too!"

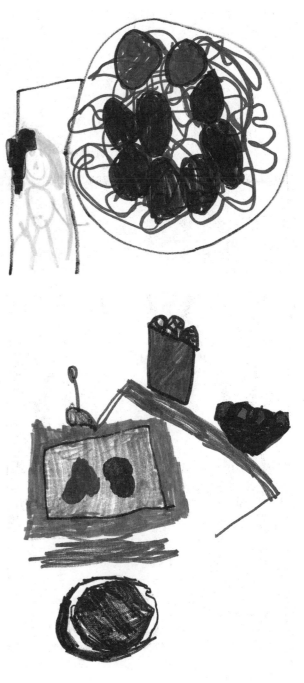

FIGURE 31–4   "I Like To Sit On the Rug and Watch TV. It Has Food On the TV. On the Table Is Popcorn and Green Olives. I Like To Eat Popcorn and Green Olives When I Watch TV."

3. Read the book *Spaghetti for Suzy.* (Coplans, P., 1993, Boston: Houghton Mifflin) Suzy liked spaghetti and ate it every day. Her mother thought she'd get tired of it, but she didn't. Her Dad thought she'd turn into a noodle soon, but she didn't. She shared the long noodles with a cat, a pig, and a dog. They brought her apples, cherries, and bananas which she ate. But they were still hungry, so Suzy invited them home to have "spaghetti for everyone."

The children listeners loved the colorful full-page pictures and soon wanted to make their own food books by drawing pictures. Once again, the teacher was surprised that not every picture included the child artist. Figure 31–3 had a role for the spaghetti itself in the child's book.

Another 4-year-old had a different idea altogether and drew a scene about her favorite foods. Her picture (Figure 31–4) is a complete story by itself, which is typical for beginners who see each picture as an entire story. But her caption, like her picture, is highly original and complex.

One of the boys wrote a complete story about a football player in one picture (Figure 31–5).

FIGURE 31–5 "A Football Player Eating Apples and Corn So He Can Be Healthy and Play Ball and Have Muscles."

A football player eating apples and corn so he can be healthy and play ball and have muscles

Logan

4. Say the words aloud as you write the caption. It is important for you to repeat the words the child dictates as you write them on the picture. Read the sentence aloud after it is completed (Neuman & Roskos, 1993, p. 214). This helps the child to see how spoken language is written. Then ask the child if he would like to read the sentence. Run your finger under the words as he reads.

REFERENCES

Neuman, S. B., & Roskos, K. A. (1993). *Language and literacy learning in the early years: An integrated approach.* Ft. Worth, TX: Harcourt.

Schickedanz, J. A. (1999). *Much more than the ABCs: Early stages of reading and writing.* Washington, DC: National Association for the Education of Young Children.

PREDICTABLE BOOKS . . .

CONCEPT

Predictable books are picture books with rhyming and repetitive words or phrases (Figure 32–1), rhythmic cadences (Figure 32–2), cumulative episodes (Figure 32–3), or sequential patterns (Figure 32–4). Children are captivated by their catchy rhythms and rhymes. They are able to chime in and follow along as an adult reads the story, and then to guess (predict) what comes next when the reader pauses. Predictable books are thus most effective in promoting young children's development of "sense of story," as well as independent reading and retelling of stories. Hearing the stories over and over, children seem to memorize the rhyming words without even trying.

FIGURE 32–1 Repetitive and Rhyming Words, Lines, and Episodes.

B Is for Bulldozer	*I Know a Rhino*
Counting Crocodiles	*Is Your Mama a Llama?*
*Flower Garden**	*Noisy Nora*

*Multicultural

Chicka Chicka Boom Boom	*Miss Mary Mack**
*How Do Dinosaurs Say Goodnight?**	*Mrs. McNosh Hangs Up Her Wash*
Going to the Zoo	*Rap a Tap Tap: Here's Bojangles, Think of That!**
K is for Kissing a Cool Kangaroo	*Silly Sally*
The Lady with the Alligator Purse	*Tikki Tikki Tembo**
Louella Mae, She's Run Away!	*Twist with a Burger, Jitter with a Bug**

*Multicultural

FIGURE 32–2 Rhythmic Cadences.

*Bein' with You This Way**	*I Know an Old Lady Who Swallowed a Fly*
Drat that Fat Cat	*Shoes from Grandpa*
Down by the Cool of the Pool	*Polar Bear, Polar Bear, What Do You Hear?*

*Multicultural

FIGURE 32–3 Cumulative Episodes.

FIGURE 32–4 Sequential
Patterns.

*Feast for Ten**	*My Name Is Alice*
Five Little Monkeys Jumping on the Bed	*My Truck Is Stuck*

*Multicultural

FIGURE 32–5 Choosing
Predictable Picture Books.

*Note: From Early literacy in preschool
and kindergarten* (p. 242) by
J. J. Beaty and L. Pratt., 2003, Upper
Saddle River, NJ: Merrill/Prentice
Hall. Adapted by permission.

- Text has repetitive and rhyming words, lines, and episodes
- Text has a rhythmic cadence
- Text has cumulative episodes
- Text uses a sequential pattern (days, numbers, letters)
- Text is brief, fast-paced, and fun
- Story features engaging human or animal characters
- Pictures clearly illustrate words

FIGURE 32–6 How Predictable
Books Help Children Learn to
Read.

*Note: From Much more than the
ABCs: Early stages of reading and
writing* by J. A. Schickendanz, 1999,
Washington, DC: National
Association for the Education of
Young Children. Adapted by
permission.

- Children can learn a simple text very quickly
- Children can anticipate what will happen next
- Children can learn to chime in with the reader on key words
- Children may read along the entire text if the book is simple
- Children can retell the book verbatim as they look at it
- Children begin to think of themselves as readers

The texts of some predictable books are like advertising jingles: so catchy you can't get them out of your head. The youngest children may still think you are reading the pictures as the story progresses, but little by little they come to realize it is the words themselves and not the pictures that tell the story. Fill your classroom with predictable books. You can't have too many. A guide for selecting predictable books from this text can be found in Figure 32–5.

As you look at the titles of these books, you will soon discover still another reason children love predictable books. They are so much fun! Whenever you see the title of a book that rhymes or sounds nonsensical, it may very well be a predictable book. Figure 32–5 lists criteria found in many, but not all, predictable books.

You may already have in mind which predictable books you want to read to your children because they are the very books both you and the children already enjoy hearing over and over. Review your books and decide which ones to start with. Do some already appeal to the children because of the rhythm and rhyming? These are the ones most easily memorized unintentionally by certain children as they hear them read again and again. If they have large font print (see LARGE FONT WORDS) as well, some of the children may recognize and remember these words when you re-read the story. For many children, predictable books are their key in learning to read (Figure 32–6).

ACTIVITIES

1. Read one of the books from the first group (repetitive & rhyming words). **Noisy Nora** (Wells, R., 1997, New York: Dial Books) tells the rhyming story of little sister Nora who is noisy because her mother and father are busy with her baby brother and sister, and nobody is noticing her. Start by showing two listeners the cover of the book, reading the title, and asking them why they think Nora

Children re-enact the story with vehicles ready to pull out the "stuck truck."

is kicking over the chair. Do they recognize the refrain repeated by her sister after every episode of Nora's mischief? ("Quiet!" said her father. "Hush!" said her mum. "Nora," said her sister, "Why are you so dumb?") Do the listeners laugh? Next time through, pause at the end of a sentence and see if they can fill in the rhyming word.

Talk about the story. Why was Nora acting the way she did? What would they have done if they were Nora? How did they like the ending? Would they like to hear the story again?

2. Read one of the books from the second group (rhythmic cadences). **Twist with a Burger, Jitter with a Bug** (Lowery, L., 1995, Boston: Houghton Mifflin) has catchy words, snappy rhythm, and collage-like characters in a riot of color that captivate most listeners. Simple text in large font words (**Dance a mambo** on the first page and **snap to a rap** on the second) alert children to the rhyme to follow (**put on your cleats and tap, tap, ___?___**).

Read this to a small group another time and have them dance or clap to the rhythm. Can they wait till you get to the funniest rhyme of all: boogie in the bathtub, hula-hula dance, rumba if you wanna, in your underpants? This book may become one of their favorites, and some children will memorize it after hearing it over and over.

3. Read one of the books from the third group (cumulative episodes). **Down by the Cool of the Pool** (Mitton, T., 2001, New York: Orchard) has a population of wildly gyrating critters: a frog (wheee!), a duck (flap), a pig (wiggle), a sheep (stamp), a cat (bound), a dog (frisk), a goat (skip and hop), a pony (prance), a donkey (drum), and a capering cow keep adding their rowdy actions to the frog's invitation to dance until they all end up in the cool of the pool. Have your listeners repeat the motion words as they accumulate one by one. Their cues this time will be the pictures of the animals.

4. Read one of the books from the fourth group (sequential patterns). **My Truck Is Stuck** (Lewis, K., 2002, New York: Hyperion) is the hilarious story of two dog drivers who get stuck in a prairie dog hole on the desert with a truckload of bones. They make a big HELP! PLEASE HELP! sign and stop every vehicle that comes along. **Tug and tow, 2 engines roar. But the truck won't go. Not one inch more.** First one vehicle hitches up and pulls, then two, three, four, five, and finally a tow truck pulls them out. But by now a parade of sneaky prairie dogs has relieved the truck of every single bone!

Listeners quickly learn to repeat the refrain, adding one more engine each time. In the meantime, have them decipher the signs on the different vehicles and the huge words in LARGE FONT.

Here is a predictable book easy to re-enact, not with child actors, but with vehicles children retrieve from the block shelves. Line 'em up, hitch 'em on, and pull! If you fill the stuck truck with crackers and let the listeners be sneaky prairie dogs, the truck will soon be empty and the children full!

REFERENCES

Beaty, J. J., & Pratt, L. (2003). *Early literacy in preschool and kindergarten.* Upper Saddle River, NJ: Merrill/Prentice Hall.

Neuman, S. B., & Roskos, K. A. (1993). *Language and literacy learning in the early years: An integrated approach.* Ft. Worth, TX: Harcourt.

Schickedanz, J. A. (1999). *Much more than the ABCs: Early stages of reading and writing.* Washington, DC: National Association for the Education of Young Children.

 PUPPETS . . .

CONCEPT

Hand puppets in an early childhood classroom can be a most exciting prop for bringing children together with books. Your puppets can be the characters in the story who invite children to come and listen. If they are girl puppets, they can be Apple Farmer Annie who grows more apples than she knows what to do with, or Silly Sally who always walks upside down, or Lola who will absolutely never eat a tomato. If they are boy puppets, they can be Lola's brother Charlie who tricks her into eating more than a tomato, or Filbert MacFee whose animal crackers turn the hospital into a zoo, or Tiny Tim who tries to eat his bathtub but it wouldn't go down his throat. Bring in some animal puppets and your children can be the cow that types, the baby owl who wants his mother, or Edward the Emu who prefers to be a snake. Excitement awaits anyone adventurous enough to put on a hand puppet!

Puppets Are Different for Young Children

Preschool children perceive puppets quite differently than teachers or older children. Three- and four-year-olds find it hard to understand the concept of a hand puppet as a doll that can speak and act. In fact, they do not treat puppets as they do their other dolls. Instead, they tend to see puppets on their hands as extensions of themselves rather than as separate objects. When they put on a hand puppet with a movable mouth, they often use it playfully to "bite" another child rather than to speak.

Puppet shows are another area of confusion for three's and four's. If they are asked to sit down in front of a puppet theater to watch a show, they tend to pop up and try to get hold of the puppets as soon as they appear. They are more interested in sticking their heads through the stage opening or running around in back to see what is going on. If they are asked to put on a puppet show themselves, they often stick their puppets far out of the stage opening, trying to touch someone in the audience.

Because their concept of "audience" is also not well developed, most young children are more comfortable using their puppets in other ways. Even the theater itself has little meaning for them at first. Left on their own, they may use a puppet theater as a pretend store. What will they sell? One group sold the puppets! But five's and six's tend to see puppets as adults do.

ACTIVITIES

1. Use puppets as book characters. When considering the use of puppets as book characters, it is essential to first select the appropriate books and re-read them to the children several times. Introduce the puppets to one or two children at a time. You will need to serve as a model puppet character yourself so the children will see how a puppet takes on a role. A puppet theater is not necessary.

When choosing books for puppet role playing, be sure that they have short, memorable texts with repetition or rhyming that can be remembered easily. Young children will be able to recall characters if there are only one or two, and the dialog between them is interesting.

Young children may need to be shown how to perform with hand puppets.

2. Obtain the puppets. It is not necessary to have a puppet that looks exactly like a specific human character, although animal puppets are best resembling specific animals. Hand puppets can be purchased or constructed by the teacher or children. Most children's book and toy stores now have hand puppets available. A good affordable source for animal puppets is in kitchen stores or kitchen departments where animal hot pad gloves are available in a variety of species. Educational supply companies have a good selection of hand puppets, such as the following from Constructive Playthings (1-800-448-4115).

Family puppets	Wild animal plush puppets
Multi-ethnic worker puppets	Farm animal plush puppets
Giant doll puppets	Forest animal plush puppets
Open-mouth puppets	Pets and pals plush puppets

Some of their puppets also go with specific books:

If You Take a Mouse to School (mouse puppet)
If You Give a Pig a Pancake (pig puppet)
If You Give a Moose a Muffin (moose puppet)
Brown Bear, Brown Bear, What do You See? (brown bear puppet)
Polar Bear, Polar Bear, What do You Hear? (polar bear puppet)

3. Make your own puppets. To make your own hand puppets with the children, obtain small brown paper bags and show children how to put a face on the outside bottom end of the bag either with markers or eye stickers. Even simpler hand puppets can be made out of a sock worn over one hand with stickers for eyes.

4. Read a simple book such as **Eat Your Peas, Louise** (Snow, P., 1985, Chicago: Children's Press) *several times.* Two characters, a father and his little girl, interact with an illustration on one page and simple text on the opposite page. The father does all the talking in rhyme and the little girl only shakes her head, refusing to eat. On the last page the father finally says "please," and Louise eats her peas. Read to a small group so everyone gets a chance to see the pictures. This, of course, is a predictable book.

Introduce the two puppets: a man and a girl. Have one of the children be the Louise puppet, and you be the father at first. Hold the little book in one hand and read with the puppet on the other. Have the Louise puppet shake her head every time you ask her a question.

Now you are ready to re-enact the story. Do it in the dramatic play center, sitting at a table and using a plate, fork, and spoon for props. Give everyone in the small group a chance to be the father and Louise as you read. These re-enactments are for the small group alone and not for an audience.

Afterwards, suggest that the group make up its own simple refusal-to-eat story to enact with puppets. Those who want can draw pictures for their own book. You can print the text for each page as children dictate it.

*5. Read a more complex book, **I Will Never Not Ever Eat a Tomato.*** (Child, L., 2000, Cambridge, MA: Candlewick) Follow the same procedure as you did in the previous story. The two puppets are the sister Lola and her brother Charlie. Both of them have dialog that you can read as children make motions with their puppets. Put out all of your plastic vegetables, fruit, and food items on the dramatic play table so that the Lola puppet can go around shaking her head at each one at first, and finally picking up each one and eating it when Charlie says things like: "These are not carrots. They are orange twiglets from Jupiter."

After they have re-enacted this story several times, some of your children may be able to repeat some of the puppet's lines.

Once again suggest that everyone draw pictures of the story (see Figure 33–1) and you will help them put it together in a book.

*6. Read another simple rhyming book, **The Lady with the Alligator Purse.*** (Westcott, N. B., 1988, Boston: Little, Brown) Children love this traditional call-for-the-doctor rhyme and soon will be shouting out in unison the words of the three puppet characters every time you pause after "the doctor said," "the nurse said," or "the lady said,"

Doctor: "mumps," "penicillin"

Nurse: "measles," "castor oil"

Lady: "nonsense," "pizza"

Afterwards, choose three puppet characters and let them act as you read. Better have pizza for their snack that day!

*7. Read the simple animal story, **Owl Babies.*** (Waddle, M. 1992, Cambridge, MA: Candlewick) The three baby owl characters who wait for mother owl to come back in the dark of the night are Sarah, Percy, and Bill. On every other page, they each have a line to speak. Bill always says "I want my

FIGURE 33–1 One Child Illustrated the Story, Calling Carrots "Power Food" Which He Printed as the Teacher Told Him the Spelling.

mama." Try to get owl hand puppets or make sock puppets from white socks with round gold stick-on eyes. Read the story several times. Then ask for three puppet volunteers from the small group to re-enact the story. Story re-enactments like this are for the group who performs them and not for an audience. If other children want to watch, tell them their turn will come another day. Once everyone in the class has had a turn, it is fine to have a total class re-enactment.

Other fine books that can be used for puppet re-enactments include

Caps for Sale	*My Crayons Talk*
Five Little Monkeys Jumping on the Bed	*Noisy Nora*
Green Eggs and Ham	*Silly Sally*
Mama, Do You Love Me?	*Where the Wild Things Are*

REFERENCES

Beaty, J. J. (1994). *Picture book storytelling.* Thompson Learning, Mason, OH.

Crepeau, I. M., & Richards, M. A. (2003). *A show of hands: Using puppets with children.* St. Paul, MN: Redleaf Press.

Davidson, J. (1996). *Emergent literacy and dramatic play in early education.* Albany, NY: Delmar.

Esch, G., & Long, E. (2002). The fabulous fun finger puppet workshop. *Young Children, 57*(1), 90–91.

Jenkins, P. D. (1980). *The magic of puppetry: A guide for those working with young children.* Upper Saddle River, NJ: Prentice Hall.

Neuman, S. B., & Roskos, K. A. (1993). *Language and literacy in the early years.* Ft. Worth, TX: Harcourt.

REBUS STORIES . . .

CONCEPT

Rebus stories will be something new for many young children. They are stories in which a little picture is substituted for one or more of the words in a sentence. For instance, in the sentence, **"I love my dog,"** the picture of a heart replaces the word **"love."** A picture of a dog replaces the word **"dog."** And in some rebuses, a picture of an eye may replace the word **"I."** In other words, rebus stories are a kind of riddle for young children as well as fun for them to figure out. Most rebus stories are in rhyme, making them predictable books with predictable sentences.

In addition to little pictures, words in some stories are also replaced by letters and numbers. For example, in the sentence **"I'll wait for you,"** the word **"for"** is replaced by the number **"4,"** and the word **"you"** is replaced by the letter **"U"** (**"I'll wait 4 U"**). Older children who can say and write most of the letters and numbers have fun writing rebus messages in code like this. Young children, on the other hand, find it easier to understand short rebus sentences with one picture to a sentence, although you may need to help them read the words of the sentence.

Strategies to Help Children Notice Words

As previously noted, young children at first see only the whole pattern of text across a page without noticing separate words. Even though you may run your finger under a particular word in a line of text for your listeners to look at, they still may have trouble recognizing separate words. Several strategies may help them begin to notice the words in a sentence. One is using books with large font words. (See LARGE FONT WORDS.) Another is using rebus books where a sentence is broken into parts by substituting a picture for a word.

ACTIVITIES

1. Read *I Love You, A Rebus Poem.* (Marzollo, J., 2000, New York: Scholastic) This simple rhyming poem has two large font lines to a page, ending with an object picture on each line. The opposite page is a full illustration of the text. (**Every** [bird picture] **loves a** [tree picture], **Every** [flower picture] **loves a** [bee picture].) Read the poem through to one or two children at a time without mentioning the pictures. Read it again stopping at the picture and asking a child to fill in the word.

Next time through, cover the pictures with your finger and see if the listeners can still say the word. If not, lift up your finger to show them the picture clue.

2. Read *I Can't Said the Ant.* (Cameron, P., 1961, New York: Scholastic) This classic rebus book, still in print, is the tale of a teapot that falls off the shelf and breaks. Each sentence in the story is a quote by a different item in the kitchen with a tiny picture of the item inserted in the middle of the sentence. ("She went kerplop!" [mop picture] said the mop.") Read it to one child at a time, running your finger under the sentence so the child can see the picture. Ask what each picture is.

During subsequent readings, pause after the phrase "said the_____" and let the child fill in the word by looking at the picture. You can cover the actual *word* with your finger if you want, but usually just pausing is enough.

After several readings, cover the *picture* with your finger and see if the listener can still say the rhyming word at the end of the sentence. Once they get the idea, children may be able to do this because the words rhyme (clatter-platter, kerplop-mop, dead-bread). But some of the words may be unfamiliar and some pictures unclear (fettle-kettle [tea kettle picture], spout-trout [fish picture]). In this case, the rhyming words may still be the clue. No matter how children respond, make it fun for them by the way you respond to their words.

Make a photo copy of one of the pages. Then cut out the little pictures (five to a page). Next, cover the little pictures on the book page with pieces of Post-It Notes.® Then lay out the five little pictures and read each sentence once again to see if the listeners can choose the right picture for the sentence. This is a long story, so reading only one or two pages at a time is the most many children can handle.

3. Use rubber stampers and a stamp pad to fill in the missing word. Obtain several rubber stampers of familiar objects from educational supply houses, scrapbook stores, or art supply departments. Write out a simple sentence for each stamper with a blank for the word represented by the stamper. (See Figure 34–1.) Write one sentence to a page on 3 pages with 3 different stampers. Have three children come to the table, find the proper stamper, and stamp the picture on the sentence. Can they read it back to you? You may have to help. They will also need to practice with the stampers to get them right-side-up and in the proper place. Have several copies of the same sentence available. Give everyone a chance.

4. Use peel-off pictures of familiar items to fill in the missing word. In the same manner, obtain peel-off pictures of familiar objects like the ones in Figure 34–2. Then write one sentence to a page with a blank for the word naming the peel-off picture. Put several peel-off pictures on the table and let children choose the proper one and stick it onto the blank space in the sentence.

5. Have children create their own rebus books. Children may want to make a rebus book of their own, either as a class project or their own personal book. Have them choose a topic such as "Our Toy Dinosaurs," "Ball Games," like the sample in Figure 34–3, or "Pets We Like." For a class book, you can write the simple sentences they say on a newsprint pad. Ask them which word should be a picture.

For their own personal rebus books, staple several sheets of paper together. Write down several sentences to a page from dictation you take. Leave spaces for words that will be replaced by pictures. Be sure you have rubber stampers or peel-off pictures for their topic.

FIGURE 34–1   Create Rebus Sentences from Rubber Stampers.

FIGURE 34–2   Create Rebus Sentences from Peel-Off Pictures.

FIGURE 34–3 Create a Story About Ball Games.

RHYMING, ALLITERATION . . .

CONCEPT

Word Play

We know that young children learn through self-discovery play. They manipulate, master and make meaning of every object in their environment if given the opportunity to play. Is it surprising, then, that young children in the early stages of language development also play with words? They try out word sounds, make up nonsense words, and repeat rhyming words over and over. Most people play little attention to this activity because it seems so inconsequential. But then we learn that many young children who have been involved in early rhyming activities such as nursery rhymes are often more successful in reading later on (Caplan & Caplan, 1983, p. 41).

Why is this? Some research tells us that to fully understand spoken language, young children need to develop *phonological awareness,* that is, an awareness of speech sounds, especially word sounds. Part of this awareness is *rhyme recognition,* the hearing and recognizing of words that sound alike, and *alliteration recognition,* the hearing and recognizing of words that start the same. Although it is not known for sure how much phonological awareness is necessary for successful reading, we do know that "children appear to hear rhyming words and words that begin the same first" and that "phonological awareness is related to reading success" (Opitz, 2000, p. 11).

Does this mean we should formally teach children to recognize rhymes? No. Just as children learn to write mainly through discovery, for the majority of children phonological awareness is more caught than taught (Opitz, p. 13). It is "caught" in homes where mothers and fathers say nursery rhymes and play pat-a-cake games with their little ones; and homes where children themselves carry on monologues in which they manipulate sounds, patterns, and meanings of words as they try to understand the language they hear.

Schwartz (1981) found that infants from 6 to 18 months often talk or sing themselves to sleep repeating rhythmic and rhyming word-sounds. On the other hand, preschool youngsters play with real words, sometimes repeating them just under their breath in nonsensical fashion: "ham-bam-lam-sam-wham-wham-wham." Listen and you may hear some (pp. 16–26).

It is "caught" in early childhood programs that feature singing, chanting, fingerplays, nursery rhymes, predictable stories, word games, and all the other informal language activities described in this text. One of the best ways to foster this word-sound awareness is by reading aloud picture books that focus on specific language elements such as rhyming and alliteration, some of which are shown in Figures 35–1 and 35–2.

FIGURE 35–1 Books That Feature Rhyming.

B Is for Bulldozer	*Flower Garden*
The Beastly Feast	*Giraffes Can't Dance*
Cat Count	*Louella Mae, She's Run Away*
Duck in a Truck	*Mice Squeak, We Speak*
Edward the Emu	*Silly Sally*
Eleanor, Ellatony, Ellencake, and Me	

ACTIVITIES

Rhyming

Choose any of these books and read it to one small group at a time following the techniques from Figure 6–2, page 19, Reading Books to Young Children. The "trick words" you will be focusing on are the rhyming words. Once the children are familiar with the book after several readings, you can proceed with the rhyming activities. These activities can be used with any rhyming book. You can create other similar games with the children.

*1. Discover the rhyming words in **B Is for Bulldozer**.* (Sobel, J., 2003, San Diego: Harcourt)

Word Detectives

Children can become word detectives if they can detect the rhyming words in this story. Have the children cover their eyes as you read two pages and listen for the words that sound alike. As in many rhyming books, they are the last word in each sentence. Here are the rhyming words from *B Is for Bulldozer.*

sky-by	sound-ground	eyes-supplies
hole-pole	pace-place	away-day
roadbed-head	controls-holes	done-fun
steel-feel	bent-cement	bloom-zooooom

Have them listen carefully and help them at first so they know what to listen for. Stick a peel-off star onto every listener who names a pair of rhymes. By the end of the book, everyone should be a word detective star.

*2. Discover the rhyming words in **Cat Count**.* (Lewin, B., 2003, New York: Holt).

Cat Collectors

Children can become Cat Collectors if they can detect the all the rhyming words on one page. This is more difficult with more than one rhyming word imbedded in every page of text. Here are *Cat Count's* collection of rhyming words.

one-fun; fat-cat	six-sticks-tricks
two-true; ballyhoo–derring-do	seven-reveling; prowling-yowling-howling
three-glee; she-he	eight-great; sedate-late
four-store; out-of-door–more	nine-fine; divine–out-of-line
five-jive-alive	ten-hen-again

Give a tiny plastic cat counter or sticker to every child who names all the rhymes on one or two pages.

*3. Discover the rhyming words in **Louella Mae, She's Run Away**.* (Alarcon K., 1997, New York: Holt).

Page Turners

Children can become Page Turners if they can fill in the blank rhyming word at the end of each page. Hold your book out to the first child who names the word. She can then turn the page to find out if she is correct. Here (**in parenthesis**) are the words:

team-(**stream**)	there-(**bear**)	ridge-(**bridge**)
be-(**tree**)	witch-(**ditch**)	Chub-(**tub**)
yarn-(**barn**)	yell-(**well**)	

FIGURE 35–2 Books That
Feature Alliteration.

Alligator Arrived with Apples: A Potluck Alphabet Feast

Eleanor, Ellatony, Ellencake, and Me

K is for Kissing a Cool Kangaroo

Potluck

Slowly, Slowly, Slowly, Said the Sloth

Alliteration

Alliteration is different than rhyming. Try not to confuse the two with the children. It is better to read books and do activities involving alliteration at a different time than those involving rhyming. Children will be listening for words that start the same. Have them close their eyes and listen to the title of each of these very different books that feature alliteration before you read the story. Can they hear the words in the following list that start with the same sound? (Figure 35–2)

1. Discover the words that start the same letter sound as in **K Is for Kissing a Cool Kangaroo.** (Andrae, G., 2003, New York: Scholastic).

Letter Leader

Children can become Letter Leaders if they can detect all the words that start with the same letter sound on a page in this book. Here are some:

b: busy, big, bumblebee	h: holiday, holding, hand
d: dragonfly, daisy, dream	m: mischievous monkey, mist
g: giant, garden, grows	p: peaceful, piglet, pear

Give every child who detects one set of these words its plastic letter to hold. Help every child in the small group to receive a letter.

2. Discover words that start the same in **Potluck.** (Shelby, A., 1991, New York: Orchard)

Lucky Potletter

Have all the children bring food that starts with the same letter as their name to the potluck (e.g., "Acton appeared with asparagus soup."). Give the child who detects these words of alliteration the letter A.

Lucky Nameletter

Play a game with each child saying his own name and the name of the food he will bring to the pretend potluck (e.g., "Jordon brings jellybeans.").

REFERENCES

Caplan, T., & Caplan, F. (1983). *The early childhood years: The 2- to 6-year-old.* New York: Putnam.

Gable, S. (1999). Promote children's literacy with poetry. *Young Children, 54*(5), 12–15.

Hohman, M. (2002). *Fee, fi, phonemic awareness: 130 prereading activities for preschoolers.* Ypsilanti, MI: High Scope Press.

Opitz, M. F. (2000). *Rhymes & reasons: Literature and language play for phonological awareness.* Portsmouth, NH: Heinemann.

Schwartz, J. I. (1981). Children's experiments with language. *Young Children, 36*(5), 16–26.

36   SCISSORS . . .

CONCEPT

To write with a writing implement requires that young children have the finger strength to hold the implement and the eye-hand coordination to control the movements of the implement. This strength and coordination develop through children's maturity and their practice using the fine muscles of their fingers, hand, wrist, and arm. Children's muscle development occurs first in the large muscles of the shoulders and arms and later down into the small muscles of the hands and fingers.

Observe how your children hold and use a writing or drawing tool. Do they hold the tool with their whole hand? Do the movements of the tool seem to come from the movement of their upper arm? If so, the marks on the paper will often be large and somewhat crude. (See photo below.) This is due to the distance between the pivot and the point of the writing. The child will have difficulty holding the tool and controlling its movements in this case. However, when he holds the writing tool in his fingers, the point of control is much closer to the end of the writing tool. (See photo on p. 114.) He is able to control what he is doing and make smaller marks (Schickedanz, 1999, p. 138).

To help children develop the necessary finger strength and eye-hand coordination to hold and control a writing tool, many small motor activities should be provided in the early childhood classroom. They include:

- Cutting with scissors
- Cutting with a knife
- Painting with a paintbrush

A 3-year-old child holds marking tool with her whole hand and moves it with her arm.

A 5-year-old child holds marking tool in a mature grip with his fingers.

- Drawing with crayons, markers, chalk
- Making puzzles
- Stringing beads
- Stirring with a spoon
- Using an egg beater
- Using squeeze bottles
- Pouring liquids
- Pounding nails with a hammer
- Using writing implements

Using scissors is perhaps one of the most effective ways to strengthen the fingers and at the same time train the eyes to follow movements of the fingers. Preschool teachers should include cutting activities on a daily basis at the beginning of the year to help youngsters prepare for the writing they will be doing.

Scissors

First, children need to find a pair of scissors that is comfortable for them from among the various types available. Be sure they are child-size classroom scissors with stainless steel blades and large enough plastic hand grips for both righties and lefties. Inexpensive toy scissors may be difficult for youngsters to hold and too dull to cut paper easily. Fiskars Scissors® have oversized, ambidextrous handles so children can hold them with multiple fingers of either hand. Safety scissors have plastic covering the entire outside of the blades.

Fiskars First Scissors® work with a spring-action that opens them after each cut. Although they are beginners' training scissors, most preschoolers can learn easily on conventional scissors. Another spring-action type is easy-grip scissors with straight handles connected by a plastic band and requiring only 50 percent of the operating energy needed for conventional scissors. They also re-open automatically. Spring-action scissors like these are especially helpful for children with limited muscular control.

As Cherry (1972) notes: "Cutting looks easy . . . but tiny immature finger muscles are not so easily directed to move in the manner necessary to guide and control their opening and closing" (p. 126). In other words, children need a great deal of practice.

ACTIVITIES

1. Use squeeze bottles and sponges. For children who have difficulty making scissors work, set up a number of activities for them to strengthen their finger muscles. Put several squeeze bottles in the water table and have them squirt water into containers. Take squeeze bottles and a bucket of water outside. Have several children fill the bottles and squirt designs on the sidewalk or a wall. Another day, fill several plastic squeeze bottles with several colors of tempera paint and have children in the art center squeeze paint designs on paper.

Cut sponges into sizes small enough for children to hold and squeeze. On your job chart, create two positions of "Sponger," children who will sponge off the art and lunch tables after use every day. Show them how to rinse their sponges and squeeze them out.

Also purchase or make fun-shape sponges of various colors (stars, hearts, butterflies, triangles, circles, arrows) and have children dip them in plates of liquid tempera paint and stamp them on paper. Have a bucket of water nearby for children to rinse out and squeeze their sponges after use in each color.

2. Set up a cutting table. Put out several pairs of scissors, along with different kinds of paper scraps and other items to be cut into small pieces: letter paper, wallpaper, construction paper, butcher paper, old greeting cards, drinking straws, coupons, wrapping paper, and ribbons. Have them collect their paper cuttings in a box for later use in art projects.

For children who need help in getting started, you can hold the paper and have them cut it. Start with a flat ribbon that you hold taut between your two hands. Have the child cut it in two, and again, and again. Then hold a flat paper the same way and have them cut it. Be patient. Once they can control the cutting, have them try holding their own paper in one hand and cutting with the other.

3. Trace and cut. The next step in learning how to cut is to cut along a line. Draw a straight line with a heavy marker across a blank paper and have the child try to follow it as she cuts. Draw more straight lines and repeat.

When this is accomplished (perhaps on another day), draw a simple tracing with a heavy marker on a blank paper and have the child cut it out (e.g., square, circle, triangle).

Learning to use scissors is an important ego-building achievement for young children.

Later have the child do her own tracing (the lid of a container or plastic dish) and cut it out. Once children are expert cutters, challenge them to cut out more complicated designs that you have drawn.

4. Cut out old magazine pictures. Fill your cutting table with old magazines that have pictures of all kinds in them. Toy companies and others may contribute catalogues of discontinued items. Have children cut them out and paste them together for a collage. At first, children may slip and cut their object in two. No problem. Have them try until they succeed. As Cherry notes: "Learning to use scissors is one of the important ego-building achievements of early childhood. The child discovers that scissors give him instant power to make changes in paper and other materials" (p. 126). They are also a precursor of using writing implements.

REFERENCES

Beaty, J. J., & Pratt, L. (2003). *Early literacy for preschool and kindergarten.* Upper Saddle River, NJ: Merrill/Prentice Hall.

Cherry, C. (1972). *Creative art for the developing child.* Belmont, CA: Fearon.

Schickedanz, J. A. (1999). *Much more than the ABCs: The early stages of reading and writing.* Washington, DC: National Association for the Education of Young Children.

SELF-CONCEPT . . .

CONCEPT

Who are these active youngsters who come bursting into your classroom every day, laughing, shouting, waving their arms, eager to enter this exciting world of learning you have provided? Do you know who they are? From the first day of their arrival you have tried to pick up hints about each of them: what they look like; how they act; what they are able to do; and what their favorite games, songs, books, and activities are. You are beginning to know them.

What about the children themselves? Do they know who they are? Strange as it may seem, many young children have not yet developed a true sense of who they are. In their earliest years, they were a part of their mothers or early caregivers. Then they became part of a family. But now they are out in the world and on their own. It is a scary situation for some of them.

You and their classmates will be helping them to develop this sense of who they are, their *self-concept,* in a positive but unobtrusive manner. Self-concept includes both the child's *self-image* or inner picture of himself, as well as his *self-esteem* or sense of worth. Although these words have been used interchangeably, they refer to different aspects of the self. Self-image, for example, is an internal image of what the child knows about her looks, gender, ethnicity, and abilities. It is descriptive, not judgmental. Self-esteem, on the other hand, refers to the child's evaluation of these aspects. Children develop their overall self-concepts by how they are treated, what people say about them, and their interactions with the people and things around them, as well as their judgmental views of what they are able to do. It is up to you as an adult in an early childhood program to make sure their vision of themselves is positive. Young children need to feel good about themselves in the classroom in order to be successful learners. Figure 37–1 lists some of the actions you can take to help every child develop this positive self-concept.

FIGURE 37–1 Promoting a Child's Positive Self-Concept.

- Accept a child unconditionally
- Smile when looking at a child
- Speak in a friendly, happy tone of voice
- Speak to each child upon arrival and departure
- Listen when a child speaks to you
- Give children choices
- Help children become involved in activities
- Help children make friends
- Discover a child's interests, favorite things
- Promote independence in reading, writing, art, computer games, tape recording, dramatic play
- Comment favorably when children succeed

ACTIVITIES

How can you promote a child's positive self-concept in the literacy activities you provide? Whether you are focusing on reading, writing, speaking, or listening, it is always good to start with a book about a child and then involve the children listeners in book extension activities. Some picture books featuring children's self-concept are listed in Figure 37–2.

1. Read *Incredible Me!* This simple rhyming story is about an exuberant little girl showing off her nose and toes, her smile and kiss, her tears and ears, her cowlick and freckles, as "the one, the only, incredible ME!" Have your small group sit close so they can see the crayon and collage pictures of ME as you read and turn the pages. Second time through the book, stop for every item the girl shows off and ask the group to show off theirs in some silly way (wiggle nose, chew with huge bites, itch, march in place, etc.).

Bring the full-length dress-up mirror to the art center and have each child stand in front of it while making a silly motion. Can they draw a picture of themselves on a nearby table with paper and crayons while holding a hand mirror to see themselves close up? Accept whatever they draw. A good example is seen in Figure 37–3. Have them dictate to you what their picture is about for an "Incredible Me" book you will all be putting together.

FIGURE 37–2   Books to Promote Children's Self-Concept.
*Multicultural

Crazy Hair Day (Saltzberg, B., 2003, Cambridge, MA: Candlewick)

*I Am Me** (Kuskin, K., 2000, New York: Simon & Schuster)

*I Can Do It Too!** (Baicker, K., 2003, Brooklyn, NY: Handprint Books)

*I Love My Hair!** (Tarpley, N. A., 1998, Boston: Little, Brown)

I'm Gonna Like Me (Curtis, J. L., 2002, New York: Joanna Colter Books)

Incredible Me! (Appelt, K., 2003, New York: HarperCollins)

FIGURE 37–3   A 4-Year-Old Girl Says: "It's Me and My Smiling Mouth."

Be sure to have a full-length mirror so children can see what they look like.

2. Read *I'm Gonna Like Me: Letting Off a Little Self-Esteem.* A boy in firefighter's hat and boots alternates with a girl dressed as a nurse in telling how they will like themselves in all sorts of situations: losing teeth, climbing on the school bus, making mistakes, being picked last, eating octopus stew. The boy strides past a mirror swinging his arms and legs. The girl listens to her father read a book, finally shouting "How about you?"

After the second reading, ask your small group what they like about themselves. What things have happened to them that were not so nice, but still they liked themselves? Can they draw a picture of themselves in one of these situations, like the one produced in Figure 37–4?

3. Read *I Can Do It Too!* Here is a colorful story with each page a different hue, the text hand-printed, and the large drawings of characters from the waist up outlined in black. A little girl tells the

FIGURE 37–4 A 4-Year-Old Girl Says: "I Got Knee Pads On So I Won't Get Hurt."

FIGURE 37–5 Sample Checklist.

INDEPENDENT SKILLS CHECKLIST

Child's Name _____ Age _____ Date _____

_____ Paints with brush	_____ Brushes teeth
_____ Mixes paints	_____ Washes hands
_____ Gets out toys	_____ Toilets
_____ Puts away toys	_____ Dresses self
_____ Picks up blocks	_____ Fastens shoes
_____ Makes puzzles	_____ Hangs up clothes
_____ Cuts with scissors	_____ Sets table
_____ Cuts with knife	_____ Pours drink
_____ Mixes dough	_____ Dishes out food
_____ Handles hammer	_____ Handles eating tools
_____ Writes name	_____ Cleans up table
_____ Signs up for turn	_____ Uses tape recorder
_____ Makes up stories	_____ Uses computer
_____ Re-enacts stories	_____ Uses camera
_____ Writes/draws in journal	_____ Speaks for puppets
_____ Sings songs	_____ Repeats fingerplays
_____ Takes on character roles	_____ Identifies rhyming words
_____ Recognizes certain words	_____ Reads signs
_____ Re-tells stories	_____ Reads books

story of all the things members of her family can do (pour juice, put on clothes, bake a cake, read a book, play a guitar, play sipping tea in a castle), after which she repeats the phrase "I can do it too!" on the opposite page. Have your listeners tell what things they can do at home.

Being independent like this makes children feel very good about themselves. What can the children do on their own in your classroom? Have a checklist of items (Figure 37–5) for you to check off as you observe each child performing the task. For children who have not accomplished certain tasks, make up games to help them or pair them with a capable buddy to show them how.

REFERENCES

Beaty, J. J. (2002). *Observing development of the young child.* Upper Saddle River, NJ: Merrill/Prentice Hall.
Marshall, H. H. (2001). Cultural influences on the development of self-concept: Updating our thinking. *Young Children, 56*(6), 19–25.

SHARED READING . . .

CONCEPT

Shared reading, a strategy more often used in older children's reading programs, can just as easily be applied to book reading with children in early childhood programs. The concept of shared reading originated in the home where an adult read to a child in an intimate setting, and the child felt free to interrupt or ask questions without ruining the story for others. Don Holdaway (1979) developed this strategy patterned after a parent's bedtime story routine. Shared reading in the classroom attempts to recreate this intimate atmosphere of the home (Neuman & Roskos, 1993, pp. 90, 238).

Most shared reading in the classroom involves using *big books* (see BIG BOOKS), the oversized editions (14 1/2 × 18 inches) of familiar books, especially *predictable books.* Teachers of young children can use big books for shared reading with small groups or the total group. The book is large enough for children to see the print as well as the pictures. When used with small groups, the children can follow along as the reader draws her finger under the text. She can stop and involve the children in a dialogue about the characters or plot. With predictable books she can ask them to guess what is coming next. The big books listed in Chapter 3, BIG BOOKS, are all predictable books from Scholastic. Big books from Constructive Playthings (1-800-448-4115) include:

Caps for Sale
The Doorbell Rang
Feathers for Lunch
I Went Walking
If You Give a Mouse a Cookie
Mean Soup
Polar Bear, Polar Bear, What Do You Hear?
Silly Sally
Stellaluna
The Three Billy-Goats Gruff

Shared reading like this takes some children to the next step in emerging into reading. With repeated readings from predictable books, they may begin to learn the lines of several stories by heart. When they realize it is the print and not the pictures that tells the story, some children may want to figure out how the print tells the reader what to say. They may point to one of the large words and ask the reader what it says. The reader in turn may point to other words the children know by heart and ask them what they say. No matter what happens in shared reading sessions, they need to be informal and fun. As Neuman and Roskos note: "In these settings, there is a spirit of collaboration as teachers and children work together in constructing meaning in stories" (p. 91).

Children feel free to ask questions in shared reading with big books.

ACTIVITIES

Some teachers prefer to place the big book on an easel facing the children while reading it. Be sure to have at least one copy of the regular-size book available for children to look at and compare with the BIG BOOK. Here is a more detailed activity for the *Five Little Monkeys Jumping on the Bed.*

1. Read the big book, **Five Little Monkeys Jumping on the Bed.** (Christelow, E., 1989, Boston: Houghton Mifflin) Show children in a small group of six the cover of the book at first and ask them what they see. Read the story all the way through without a pause. Next time through, ask the children to repeat in unison what the doctor says the five different times: "No more monkeys jumping on the bed!" Count off the children 1 through 5 to represent the monkeys. Ask the sixth child to be the mother.

Next time through, have the five children stand up and jump up and down as described in the book. When one falls down, have that child sit down. At the same time, have all the children repeat the doctor's words. By now, most of the children will know the story by heart.

Have them remain seated this time and say as much of the story in unison as they can. Finally, close the book and see if they can say the story in unison without the book while jumping.

2. Look for word recognition from **Five Little Monkeys.** Another day, print out six signs on cards saying "MONKEY #1," "MONKEY #2," "MONKEY #3," "MONKEY #4," "MONKEY #5," "MOTHER." With the children seated, ask if anyone can find the word "monkey" in the book as you read it together. Give that child Monkey #1 to hold. Continue reading and ask the same question each time you come to the same word. Can they tell the difference between the word "monkey" and "mother"?

Read this book to other groups of six children until everyone has had the chance to learn the story and pick out the words.

REFERENCES

Beaty, J. J., & Pratt, L. (2003). *Early literacy in preschool and kindergarten.* Upper Saddle River, NJ: Merrill/Prentice Hall.

Neuman, S. B., & Roskos, K. A. (1993). *Language and literacy in the early years: An integrated approach.* Ft. Worth, TX: Harcourt.

SINGING . . .

CONCEPT

Singing and speaking have similar roots. They both evolve from the early vocalizations of infants and young children. Most children learn to speak by hearing language spoken around them. They could just as easily learn to sing by hearing songs sung around them. This is certainly the case among many non-Western and indigenous people who make singing a natural part of their life. If the children in your class are not used to singing, you can introduce them to this special skill that can be just as important in learning to read as speaking is.

Singing helps children to develop the rhythmic patterns of language and to recognize the sounds of rhyming words. It taps into the right hemisphere of the brain which operates both the music and memory functions. It connects the right hemisphere with the left hemisphere which operates speaking and reading. The steady beat of singing develops pathways in the brain that appear to be essential for learning, especially as related to reading (Snyder, 1997, pp. 169–170).

Singing is a natural language for young children that speaks to them in tones they can relate to. Sing a song in the classroom and you quickly have everyone's attention. Waltz around the room as you sing and the children will soon be up on their feet following you. Children perk up and listen when you sing a musical transition or give directions in song. Are you having trouble getting children to pick up the blocks? Sing them a challenge like this to the tune of "Here We Go Round the Mulberry Bush."

> Who can pick the blocks up now,
> Blocks up now, blocks up now?
> Who can pick the blocks up now,
> Before I finish singing? (repeat)

Why do songs seem to work better than words? Perhaps it is the melodic tones that children respond to, making things sound like fun rather than a chore. Maybe it is the rhythm that resonates with children's own heartbeat. Whatever the reason, teachers of young children know that music makes a difference in the classroom. Snyder (1997) says, "There is evidence that music is pre-literate, emerging before word language, and actually encompassing word language through common expressive features of pitch, duration, stress, tone, color, dynamics, tempo, and phrase, and sometimes use of words" (p. 166).

For music to be meaningful, there must be active involvement by the children in which they take part in the singing while interacting with others. Hands-on, direct musical experiences are best in which children listen to, engage in, and learn from the singing. Most observers of young children will tell you it is the music-maker who gets the most from the musical experience. This means that not only you, but also the children should originate their own singing. Neely (2001) suggests that adults and children can engage in *musical conversations* "in which children make learning connections through their music making" (p. 35).

ACTIVITIES

1. What if you are not a singer? What if you are not a singer and can't carry a tune? Try it anyway. It's important for the children. Start with a monotone. Sing (don't say):

> Rain, <u>rain,</u> go a-<u>way,</u>
>
> Come a-<u>gain</u> another <u>day;</u>
>
> All the <u>children</u> want to <u>play.</u>

Now drop down a tone when you come to the underlined words. Sing it, don't say it. There! You are singing!

Take home recordings of children's traditional nursery songs and play them over and over. Try singing along with them. Choose the ones that are easiest for you to use with the children. Here are some traditional titles:

Alphabet Song[#]	*Jack and Jill*[#]
Are You Sleeping?	*John Jacob Jingleheimer Schmidt*[#]
Do the Hokey, Pokey	*London Bridge Is Falling Down*
Down by the Station[#]	*Mary Had a Little Lamb*
Eentsy Weentsy Spider[#]	*Ring Around the Rosy*[#]
Go in and Out the Windows	*Row, Row, Row Your Boat*
Here We Go Looby Loo	*Shoo Fly*
Here We Go Round the Mulberry Bush[#]	*Three Blind Mice*
Hickory Dickory Dock[#]	*Twinkle, Twinkle Little Star*[#]
If You're Happy[#]	*Wheels on the Bus*
I'm a Little Teapot[#]	*Where Is Thumbkin*[#]
Head and Shoulders[#]	

Songs with a pound sign are found in the songbook *Wee Sing: Children's Songs and Fingerplays* (Beall & Nipp, 1981, Los Angeles: Price/Stern/Sloan). A CD or cassette, along with the songbook, is available through Lakeshore Learning Materials (1-800-778-4456). Other records, CDs, and cassettes from Lakeshore with traditional songs include *Classic Nursery Rhymes, Classroom Song Bank,* and *Alphabet Songs* in which every letter of the alphabet has its own song with original words sung to the tune of a familiar nursery rhyme (H for Hungry Hippos is sung to *Twinkle, Twinkle Little Star*). The recording is accompanied by a big-book–size poster for each letter, showing a picture and the lyrics to the song.

2. Make "musical conversations" from old songs with new words. Now that you have a repertoire of familiar songs to sing with the children (even two is a repertoire!), you can begin your musical conversations. First sing the song with the children over and over using the traditional words until you know they are familiar with the tune. Now you can use that tune for your musical conversations. What will you talk about? What about feelings, hunger, waiting, weather, sleepiness, listening, congratulations, and special occasions?

One teacher chose to use the tune for *Here We Go Round the Mulberry Bush* every time the class got ready to go outside. They soon came to recognize the tune as a signal to get ready. Sometimes the teacher would hum the tune or whistle it. They even recognized the get-ready signal when the teacher tapped it on a drum without saying a word. She used different words whenever the occasion called for them.

> Now it's time to go outside, go outside, go outside;
>
> Now it's time to go outside;
>
> Everyone get ready.

or

> Allison and Kyle are ready now, ready now, ready now;
> Yolanda and Keshawn are ready now,
> When will you be ready?

She encouraged the children to sing back answers to her.

> Me and Brandon are ready now, ready now, ready now,
> Melissa and Jennifer are ready now,
> Everybody else is not!

3. *Help children initiate singing.* Too often it is the teacher who starts the singing. You need to encourage children to sing when they feel like it by doing it yourself at first (Tune: *Row, Row, Row Your Boat*).

> Help, help, help me please,
> Help me find the guinea pig,
> Scurrying, scurrying,
> Scampering, scampering
> He is not a skinny pig.

Play song recordings for the children if you feel it is necessary, but afterwards have them make up their own words. Music should be informal and fun. If it is, children will enjoy singing on their own.

Children sing on their own when music is informal and fun.

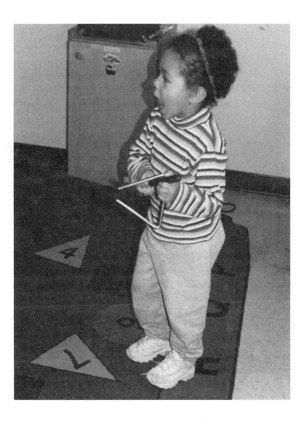

REFERENCES

Beaty, J. J., & Pratt, L. (2003). *Early literacy in preschool and kindergarten.* Upper Saddle River, NJ: Merrill/Prentice Hall.

Hildebrandt, C. (1998). Creativity in music and early childhood. *Young Children, 53*(6), 68–73.

Moravcik, E. (2000). Music all the livelong day. *Young Children, 55*(4), 27–29.

Neelly, L. P. (2001). Developmentally appropriate music practice: Children learn what they live. *Young Children, 56*(3), 32–37.

Palmer, H. (2001). The music, movement, and learning connection. *Young Children, 56*(95), 13–17.

Snyder, S. (1997). Developing musical intelligence: Why & how. *Early Childhood Education Journal, 24*(3), 165–171.

40 SONG STORYBOOKS . . .

CONCEPT

One of the most effective ways of making a connection between singing, a right brain function, and reading, a left brain function, is through *song storybooks*. Song storybooks are picture books whose stories are told in the words of children's favorite songs. Such books are predictable because children already know the words of the songs by heart. Now they will be able to see them illustrated in pictures and in print. What fun! A line from the song is illustrated on each page with pictures of the song characters enacting what the words describe. Most of these books have the musical notations on the front or back pages. Children are delighted to see a song they know in the pages of a book. Can they recognize any of the printed words?

Jalongo and Ribblett (1997) say: "When children participate in read aloud/sing aloud sessions with song picture books, they are involved in authentic, holistic literacy experiences, rather than task-focused instruction that breaks up reading into discrete skills" (p. 16). Moreover, children have fun participating in the experience both by singing and eventually reading the words, and will want to repeat it. Some of the books you may want your children to experience include those in Figure 40–1. Those with an asterisk are also available in big book as well as regular book size.

Some can be purchased from either Lakeshore or Constructive Playthings. A few come with a cassette or CD of the music. But if children know the tune and words, it is more effective for them to sing the songs without musical accompaniment as you turn the book pages.

FIGURE 40–1 Song Storybooks.
*Also available as big book

Down by the Station*
The Farmer in the Dell
Fiddle-I-Fee
If You're Happy and You Know It
Miss Mary Mack
I'm a Little Teapot*
Itsy Bitsy Spider*
Mary Had a Little Lamb
Old MacDonald Had a Farm*
Skip to My Lou
There Was an Old Lady Who Swallowed a Fly*
This Old Man*
Twinkle, Twinkle Little Star*
The Wheels on the Bus*

Children can sing the words of song storybooks and later see them in print.

ACTIVITIES

1. Read *Fiddle-I-Fee: A Farmyard Song for the Very Young.* (Sweet, M., 1992, Boston: Little, Brown) This rhyming cumulative tale can become one of the children's favorites if you start with the singing of the simple three-note song (as shown on the last two pages) before even showing the book to the children.

> I had a cat,
>
> And the cat pleased me;
>
> I fed my cat under yonder tree;
>
> Cat went fiddle-i-fee.

The farm child also had a hen who went *chipsy-chopsy,* a duck who went *quack-quack,* a goose who went *swishy-swashy,* a dog who went *bow-wow,* a sheep who went *baa-baa,* a pig who went *griffy-gruffy,* a goat who went *bleat-bleat,* and a cow who went *moo-moo.* Each time a new animal is added, children must sing what each of the others said in order, ending with the cat who plays the fiddle. Children can have fun repeating the lines: *I had a _____, And the _____ pleased me; I fed my _____ under yonder tree; _____ went _____.* They especially enjoy saying the funny sounds.

It is always surprising how quickly young children learn the tune and words that are fun for them. Won't they be surprised when you show your small groups what the words look like in the pictures of this book! First time through, read the words to them, turning the pages one by one. The children can be encouraged to participate in this predictable book by saying the name of the animal who comes next (*I had a _____*) before each page is turned. The animals parade behind the child in the illustrations, stepping deftly on the stones across a pond, across a bridge, on top of a fence, and down a path to the farm house where a picnic spread out on a huge outdoor table awaits all of them.

Next time through, sing the song running your finger under the words as you sing. Soon most of the children will join in the song because the tune is so catchy. Have them slow down enough to follow the words.

Who would like to say the words of the cat? Hen? Duck? Goose? Dog? Sheep? Pig? Goat? Cow? Each time the children sing the song, you can turn the pages, but stop for the chosen child to sing his animal's words. If you have toy animals in the block center to represent these, each child can hold his animal, as well.

Another time, have the children exchange animals and their sounds. Be sure to spend a few moments showing the child the book words that she is singing for her animal. If this is the cat from *Hey Diddle, Diddle, the Cat and His Fiddle,* wouldn't it be fun to have a violin player visit the class and play *Fiddle-I-Fee?*

2. Read *Skip to My Lou. (Westcott, N. B., 1989, Boston: Little, Brown)* Here is another traditional song in book form about the farm animals who cause all sorts of mischief in the farmhouse when the farmer is away. The farmer's boy tries to shoo away the "flies in the sugarbowl," but that's just the start of it. There are "cats in the buttermilk," "pigs in the parlor," "cows in the kitchen," "roosters in the pantry," and "sheep in the bathtub," all having a hullabaloo in the riotous illustrations. So what can the poor boy do? Why, join in, of course.

Have your children sing the song without seeing the book until they are familiar with it. Then read the book to one small group at a time. Have them investigate the hilarious hodgepodge of details on every page. How many cats get into the buttermilk? Can anyone find 12? What are the pigs in the parlor up to? And sheep snorkeling in the bathtub? Next, sing the song together as you turn the pages.

Play a circle singing game with the various animals acting out their roles in the center and the rest of the class singing and clapping out the catchy rhythm. At the same time remember, it is the words of the book that are most important in this activity. Can any children put their finger on words like "sugarbowl," "buttermilk," "parlor," or "pantry"? Write these words on cards and have the appropriate animal actors wave them around when it is their turn.

3. Read *Mary Had a Little Lamb.* (Hoberman, M. A., 2003, Boston: Little, Brown) Here is the latest version of this traditional nursery rhyme song with illustrations showing the lamb being scrubbed in an inflated swimming pool to make its fleece "white as snow." The verses continue with the lamb not only following Mary to school but joining in a kickball game at recess, eating lunch, and learning to read and write.

For a change, read the book first with all the new verses added. Then sing the song over and over with the children until they learn it by heart. Next have your small listening group choose parts: Mary, the lamb, two children. As you read the verses, have the children act out their parts. Finally, sing the song together with different actors doing what the words say.

The last page of the book has five more activities to keep your children involved. Be sure they make up some new funny verses of their own and some new rules the lamb must follow when in school.

REFERENCES

Beaty, J. J., & Pratt, L. (2003). *Early literacy in preschool and kindergarten.* Upper Saddle River, NJ: Merrill/Prentice Hall.

Jalongo, M. R., & Ribblett, D. M. (1997). Using song picture books to support emergent literacy. *Childhood Education, 74*(1), 15–28.

SOUND WORDS . . .

CONCEPT

Sound words are words that describe sounds: sounds made by animals, by vehicles, by objects, or by people. Sound words are important in children's development of phonemic awareness. For this particular strategy, you should be looking for books that have one or two words describing sounds like these: *Gr-r-r-r* for a growl, *cluck-cluck* for a hen, *snip* for scissors, *boom* for a bass drum, or similar words. Children enjoy making these sounds when you come to the place in a book where they occur. Even more important is the fact that children may be able to identify the words themselves when they come to them in a book.

Identifying words and saying them is at the very core of learning to read. Look through your library to see if any of your picture books are full of sound words. Sometimes the title will suggest that the story uses these words. Next time you purchase books, be sure some of them include sound words like the books in Figure 41–1.

ACTIVITIES

1. Read *Baby-O.* (Carlstrom, N. W., 1992, Boston: Little, Brown) This joyful Caribbean story of a bus bouncing through the countryside, picking up members of a family and their produce to take to market is actually another song storybook. But if you read it to the children instead of singing it, they may more easily find the following sound words:

chickens: *chucka-chucka*	Sister: *pika-pika*
Mama: *wusha-wusha*	Granny: *plesh-plesh*
Brother: *tomatoma-tomatoma*	Papa: *dippa-dippa*
Pappy: *kongada-kongada*	Jitney: *putta putta clank clank*

Go through the story again with a small group and have them repeat any of these sound words they remember.

FIGURE 41–1 Books with Sound Words.

*Baby-O!**

*Cock-A-Doodle Doo!**

Down by the Cool of the Pool

*Hush!**

If You're Happy and You Know It!

*Mice Squeak, We Speak**

Off We Go!

Old MacDonald Had a Farm

Polar Bear, Polar Bear, What Do You Hear?

*Multicultural

When children are familiar with the story and the words, have each child in your group of eight choose a sound word to make when you come to it in your reading.

Finally, on another day, read the book to two children on either side of you. Can they put their fingers on any of the sound words you read?

2. Read *Cock-A-Doodle-Doo! What Does It Sound Like To You?* (Robinson, M., 1993, New York: Workman Publishing) Familiar sounds in English do not sound the same in other languages. This book tells how Spanish roosters cry KEE-KEE-REE-KEE, and Japanese roosters, KOH-KEH-KOH-KOH. Trains that say CHOO-CHOO in English say TOOT TOOT in French and STOOK STOOK in Russian. American dogs bark BOW WOW, Greek dogs bark GUV GUV, and Chinese WO WO. Read this book to individuals or pairs so they can sit close and see the words coming out of the mouths of animals like the Swahili frog (KROO KROO), the Japanese frog (GEDO GEDO), and the German frog (KWOK KWOK). Have them guess what the bees say in English (BZZZ). Then read their sound in Hebrew (ZMMM) or Indian (HMMM). Hammers that bang and water that drips sound very different in Spain, Portugal, Africa, and Russia. Don't expect the children to memorize all of these different sounds, but let them repeat the sounds after you read them.

3. Read *Hush! A Thai Lullaby.* (Minfong Ho, H., 1996, New York: Orchard Books) Read to individuals or pairs who will sit close enough to see the action in this unusual book. A Thai mother tries to hush the animals' sounds around her thatched house while her baby is sleeping in a woven hammock. TUK-GHAA peeps the long-tailed lizard, JEED-JEED squeaks the fat gray mouse, UUT-UUT sniffles the muddy pig, JIAK-JIAK cries the loose-limbed monkey, MAAAU says the water buffalo, and HOOM-PRAA shrieks the elephant. But each time the text shows the mother shushing an animal because her baby's sleeping, the illustrations show the baby sneaking here and there behind the mother's back. Finally everyone is asleep but baby in his hammock, playing with his toes. As you say these strange sound words, put your finger under them and have your listeners repeat the sounds.

4. Read *Mice Squeak, We Speak.* (dePaola, T., 1997, New York: Putnam) This simple rhyming book shows three multicultural children telling what different animals say in a two-word sentence at the bottom of each page, concluding with their own speech. Play a magic-word game with your listeners each time you read this story. Tell them what the magic word is, ask them to listen for it, and then they must quickly perform the sound. For example, when they hear the magic word *roar*, they should all roar; for *neigh*, everyone should make a horse neighing sound.

Once they are familiar with the book, have children sit so they can see the pages and ask one at a time to see if they can point to the sound word you have just read.

5. Read *Polar Bear, Polar Bear, What Do You Hear?* (Martin, B., 1991, New York: Holt) Read this rhyming predictable book to a small group for a shared reading experience. It is available as both a regular size and big book. Large double-page pictures of a polar bear, lion, hippo, flamingo, zebra, boa constrictor, elephant, leopard, peacock, and walrus each hear the next animal roaring, snorting, fluting, braying, hissing, trumpeting, snarling, yelping, and bellowing. Finally, on the last page the zookeeper hears children making all these sounds. Children may not know the meaning of the sound words, but they will enjoy making up each of these sounds.

Have children make and color headbands with animal ears for each of the animals. They can wear them every time you read the book. Run your finger under the lines of the big book as you read it. Have children repeat the lines they know in unison. When you come to a sound word, have the children with that animal's headband make the sound. Another time, point to a word that says the name of an animal to see who knows it. Picture clues should help.

REFERENCES

Beaty, J. J., & Pratt, L. (2003). *Early literacy in preschool and kindergarten.* Upper Saddle River, NJ: Merrill/Prentice Hall.

Hohman, M. (2002). *Fee, fi, phonemic awareness: 130 prereading activities for preschoolers.* Ypsilanti, MI: High/Scope Press.

Neuman, S. B., & Roskos, K. A. (1993). *Language and literacy in the early years: An integrated approach.* Ft. Worth, TX: Harcourt.

STORY RE-ENACTMENTS . . .

CONCEPT

One of the best ways to make picture books memorable for children is through story re-enactments. Story re-enactments are informal, on-the-spot dramas performed by the children about a familiar story while you are reading it. The drama is for the children themselves and not an audience—unless the children want one. They can be simple stories having only a few characters, like *Owl Babies* with its three baby owls and the mother. Or they can be quite complex, like *Giraffes Can't Dance* with a whole collection of jungle animals.

Books best suited for story re-enactments are those with several characters who talk, a lot of action, and a minimum of text. Rhyming and predictable books are best because they help children memorize the words. It is not necessary for children to repeat all the dialogue in the text, for you will be reading it as they act it out. But most children want to say a few words or at least make animal sounds. Costumes also are not necessary, but again, children like to wear hats, animal ears they have made, or at least a sign around their necks telling who they are. Some books well suited to story re-enactments are found in Figure 42–1. If children want to re-enact more complex stories, you can adapt them. Pretending is serious business for young children, and to be able to pretend about the story in a book gives them great satisfaction.

What if more than one child wants the part of a character? Simply re-enact the story again with a different set of characters. The more you do it, the better. Ishee and Goldhaber (1990) tell how their children performed *The Three Bears* 27 times in 4 days! Remember that repetition (mastery) is one of the 3-Ms of Self-Discovery (manipulation, mastery, and meaning) which most children use to make new experiences part of their repertoire. (See ALPHABET.) Repeating the re-enactment also helps shy children develop the courage to participate.

What about scenery? Story re-enactments are not staged plays and scenery or props are not necessary. However, it makes sense to use labeled chairs or tables to represent objects in the story when appropriate. These little dramas need to be as simple as possible so that children can perform them in an impromptu manner without a fuss. What if children forget their lines or their actions? Of course they will

FIGURE 42–1 Books for Story Re-Enactments.

- Caps for Sale
- Drat That Fat Cat
- Edward the Emu
- Giraffes Can't Dance
- Is Your Mama a Llama?
- Louella Mae, She's Run Away
- Owl Babies
- Silly Sally
- Sometimes I'm Bombaloo
- The Three Bears
- The Three Billy Goats Gruff

at first because they perform without practicing. It is the *process* of making a story come alive that is most important, not the *product* of a finished play. Eventually, after you have read the story many times, certain children may have memorized the words and can even replace you as the "reader." Important benefits are gained by children from story re-enactments when they learn:

- That words, not pictures, tell the story
- New words, new meanings of words
- A better "sense of story"
- That stories can come alive through acting
- That reading can be extended to other areas of the classroom
- That they will want to re-read the book
- That they can create their own stories
- That reading can be fun

ACTIVITIES

1. Read and re-enact *Owl Babies.* (Waddell, M., 1992, Cambridge, MA: Candlewick) This story needs to be a familiar one for the children, and also a favorite. They will remember the three frightened little owl babies—Sarah, Percy, and Bill—who huddle together in their tree-hole nest when their mother goes out at night hunting for food. At last they come out and wait on the tree branches, finally all huddling together on Sarah's branch, and then Mommy returns.

Have the children choose the characters of the owls and the mother. Give each a sign to wear with their names (or they can make their own). Put out a small rug for the nest, and three chairs for the branches. The rest of the children are the audience.

Read the story, having the owl-actors huddle together on the rug, come out and sit on the chairs, push the chairs together when they move over to Sarah's branch, and say their simple parts if they want. They can repeat them after you, if they want. The Bill character always says the same words, "I want my mommy!" until the end when he says, "I love my mommy!" Have the mother owl swoop in when it is her turn. Don't forget to have the audience clap at the end.

Ask the children afterwards if they noticed that the book pictures show the three owls as being three different sizes. That is because owls lay their eggs a day apart and not all at once. One day older makes a size difference in owls. If children want to repeat the re-enactment right away, you'll know it was successful. If they want to make up their own baby owl story, all the better.

2. Read and re-enact *Giraffes Can't Dance.* (Andrae, G., 1999, New York: Orchard) All the children in your group or class can play the many jungle animal roles in this rhyming story after they become familiar with it. Gerald Giraffe was good at standing still and munching leaves off trees, but when he tried to run around, his knees buckled. He knew he would be unable to dance at the annual Jungle Dance. The warthogs were waltzing, the rhinos rock n' rolled, the lions tangoed, the chimps did the cha-cha, and the baboons reeled off a Scottish reel. But when Gerald tried to take a turn, they laughed him off the jungle floor. Back among the trees, a cricket told him he needed to find his own music: the swaying grass, the magic moon. Soon Gerald found his body shuffling, swaying, and dancing. The other animals said it was a miracle. Gerald said "We all can dance when we find music that we love."

Have the children choose what animal they want to be and let them each make their moves to the snappy background music or jungle drums as you read the story. When Gerald finally takes the floor, have the others sit in a circle around him as he dances.

Your characters may want to make head bands with animal ears to wear for the re-enactment. Another time have a small group re-enact the story with only six children taking animal parts by dancing with large animal hand puppets. Lakeshore Learning Materials (1-800-778-4456) can supply large plush Big Mouth Jungle Puppets (Monkey, Rhino, Giraffe, Panda, Alligator, and Tiger)

This boy plays Gerald's swaying jungle dance as the story unfolds.

very reasonably, or children can make their own from paper bags or socks. You can adapt the story to the animals you have.

Another time, have the characters choose different types of music to dance to just as Gerald did. Try out several musical tapes or rhythms on xylophones or drums. Can the children make their own music with rhythm instruments?

REFERENCES

Beaty, J. J., & Pratt, L. (2003). *Early literacy in preschool and kindergarten.* Upper Saddle River, NJ: Merrill/Prentice Hall.

Davidson, J. (1996). *Emergent literacy and dramatic play in early education.* Albany, NY: Delmar.

Ishee, N., & Goldhaber, J. (1990). Story re-enactment: Let the play begin! *Young Children, 45*(3), 70–75.

Rowe, D. W. (2000). Bringing books to life: The role of book-related dramatic play in young children's literacy learning. In Roskos, K. A., & Christie, J. F. (Eds.), *Play and Literacy in Early Childhood.* Mahwah, NJ: Lawrence Erlbaum Associates.

STORYTELLING . . .

CONCEPT

Storytelling differs from story reading aloud in several significant ways. The story being told comes from the teller rather than the words in a book. The story depends on the teller's use of words and gestures rather than on the text and illustrations of a picture book. Furthermore, the teller concentrates on the audience rather than on a book. Both forms of story presentation are important for young children's early literacy learning. But why would a teacher want to go through the process of learning to tell a story when all she needs to do is pick up a picture book and read it aloud? Storytelling has its own advantages, such as

- Frees the teller to engage children's attention by being more animated.
- Makes the teller more aware of children's reactions to the story.
- Teller can project more of herself into the story (gestures, expression).
- Teller can tailor the story to children's attention span.
- Teller can elicit individual and group participation more easily.
- Telling can stimulate children to make their own mental images, rather than relying on book illustrations.
- Adult telling can serve as a model for children to emulate in their own storytelling.
- Telling can become the vehicle for prereading children to present stories.
- Children love it!

Picture Book Storytelling

Because this text is focused on bringing young children together with books, the storytelling discussed here will come from stories in appropriate picture books in the classroom. These books should be the ones with the following characteristics:

1. PLOT: plot incidents that happen in an easily remembered order
2. CHARACTERS: one or two interesting characters who speak
3. REPETITION: words, phrases, or incidents that are repeated

You will not be using the book itself in your storytelling, so choose books that are not too long or complicated and can easily be remembered. Books with folktale-like plots where three things happen in a certain order are a good choice. But any book you really like can be adapted to this sort of formula for telling. You can use the actual words from the book (especially repeated words) or tell the story in your own words. Some of the books you might choose include those in Figure 43–1.

FIGURE 43–1   Picture Books for
Storytelling.

Blueberries for Sal	*It's Simple, Said Simon**
Caps for Sale	*Juan Bobo Goes to Work**
Click, Clack, Moo, Cows that Type	*Owl Babies*
Drat That Fat Cat	*Silly Sally*
Goldilocks and the Three Bears	*The Three Billy Goats Gruff*
Giraffes Can't Dance	*Whistle for Willie**

*Multicultural

ACTIVITIES

1. Tell the story from **Drat That Fat Cat.** (Thompson, P., 2003, New York: Arthur A. Levine Books)
Here is a story children really enjoy—not about the lady who swallows a fly, but about the cat who
swallows a lady! You will be telling the story before you show the book to the children. But first you
need to prepare in the following manner:

1. Read the book to yourself several times aloud.

2. Outline the story on a file card telling the main incidents and dialogue.

   a. Cat meets a rat and eats him ("squeak, squeak, squeak").

   b. Cat meets a duck and eats him ("quack, quack, quack").

   c. Cat meets a dog and eats him ("woof, woof, woof").

   d. Cat meets an old lady and eats her. ("Drat that fat cat!").

   e. Cat swallows a bee whole. (The bee stings him. "Oow!")

   f. Cat goes "Hic!" five times; each time out pops bee, rat, duck, dog, and lady.

3. Repeated words: "But was that cat fat enough? **No, he was not!** So he padded along the path
   in search of food."

Put the book away and practice telling the story aloud privately. Then tell it to the whole class. Start
with the first line of the book and go on from there. ("Once there was a cat, a fat, fat cat.") Use
different voice tones for the sounds of the animals inside the cat. Have the children answer in
unison, **No, he was not!** each time you ask the question, "But was that cat fat enough?" Be sure to
use gestures of eating, swallowing, and slapping at the bee. Children will love it. They will want you
to do it again. And then imagine their delight when you show them the book. Put it in the book
center and let them investigate it on their own.

This story can easily be adapted to any group of animals (jungle animals, dinosaurs, farm animals).

2. Tell the story from **It's Simple, Said Simon.** (Hoberman, M., 2001, New York: Knopf) Here is
another folktale-like story children enjoy about the Latino boy who meets various talking animals
who ask him to do what they do, which he does. Outline the story as previously and practice it
before you tell it to the class or show them the book. Be sure to use gestures, expression, and
animation as you tell the tale.

1. Read the book to yourself several times aloud.

2. Outline the story on a file card telling the main incidents and dialogue

   a. Simon meets dog (growls).

   b. Simon meets cat (stretches).

   c. Simon meets horse (jumps).

   d. Simon meets tiger (growls, stretches, jumps).

   e. Simon jumps on tiger's back, rides to river for a drink.

   f. Simon rides out into river, jumps off tiger, and swims home.

3. Repeated words: "Very good" say the animals. "It's simple, says Simon."

Children can retell favorite stories to a partner.

After you have told the story several times over, ask who would like to retell this story. Give everyone a chance who wants one.

3. Encourage children to retell this story or any story they know. As Isbell (2002) notes, for children to tell a story helps them understand how the story works, what phrases are repeated, and what the sequence of action is (p. 27). Every time they retell a story, they build on their knowledge of what goes into a story and how to make it exciting with their voice and gestures. Do not push children to tell stories or try to tell them perfectly. Accept whatever they do. Storytelling should be fun and exciting for everyone involved.

Children often like to hold the book while they tell the story. They can retell their stories to a small group or even to a partner. The total class is often too overpowering for beginning storytellers. Some will prefer to tell their stories to a tape recorder and listen to them later.

Tape record any of the stories children retell to the group if they agree. They can be transcribed and written into a personal book for the child, or played later for others to enjoy.

REFERENCES

Beaty, J. J. (1994). *Picture book storytelling: Literature activities for young children.* Ft. Worth, TX: Harcourt.

Hall, N. (1998). *Young children as storytellers.* In R. E. Campbell (Ed.), *Facilitating preschool literacy,* (pp. 84–99), Newark, DE: International Reading Association.

Isbell, R. T. (2002). Telling and retelling stories: Learning language and literacy. *Young Children, 57*(2), 26–30.

Zeece, P. D. (1997). Bringing books to life: Literature-based storytelling. *Early Childhood Education Journal, 25*(1), 39–43.

 **SYLLABLES . . .**

CONCEPT

Recognizing the syllables of words is a part of the broader concept of *phonemic awareness,* which is related to children's reading success. Phonemic awareness itself is the ability to recognize and manipulate the individual sounds in words, the phonemes. Wasik (2001) tells us: "Children who know how to manipulate sounds in words at an early age have greater success in learning to read in the 1st and 2nd grades" (p. 129). This is not *phonics,* but instead the oral recognition of sounds in words. Young children can be aware of sounds without knowing the letter name for the sound. For instance, children who recognize words that rhyme or words that begin the same are demonstrating phonemic awareness, an aspect of phonological awareness. (See RHYMING, ALLITERATION.)

Children seem to hear rhyming words and alliteration first. Next comes the ability to hear, blend, and isolate individual sounds in words (Opitz, 2000, p. 11). This ability is more caught than taught for most children. Children need to experience a rich classroom environment that includes reading aloud, storytelling, singing, chanting, nursery rhymes, and all kinds of word play. Play with breaking words into syllables helps to promote children's phonemic awareness: that words are made up of sounds.

The experiences you arrange to help children learn to segment words into their separate sounds should first of all be fun and not isolated drill activities. They should be a part of your everyday oral literacy activities. Clapping, drumming, and rhythmic activities are especially well suited to helping children recognize syllables orally.

ACTIVITIES

1. Name-clapping At morning circle time, go around the circle asking each child to say his or her name while the rest listen carefully. You may have to ask, "Say it again, Brandon. Okay. Did everyone hear the two sounds in Brandon's name? Bran-don? Let's say and clap Brandon's name: Bran-don!

"Who's next? Yes, Jessica. Say your name slowly, Jessica, and let's listen for the sounds in your name. Jes-si-ca. How many sounds? Yes, three sounds. Let's say and clap Jessica's name."

Once you have clapped out everyone's name, you can have the children say "hello" to each child by clapping hel-lo and then their name. See if you can trick anyone by pointing to children here and there instead of in order.

Finally, have children clap out the syllables of each name without saying the name. Good. Now you can be the clapper and try to trick them again. Clap once without saying a name and ask them whose name you just clapped. Does anyone recognize "Mark"? Clap 3 times. Whose name is that? Yes, Jes-si-ca, but also Jer-em-y, Greg-or-y, La-shan-dra, and Sa-man-tha. Clap 2 times. Does anyone recognize Ma-son or Jef-frey or Kay-la or Me-gan or Ke-shawn? Clap 4 times. Who can that be? What about An-ton-i-o or Al-ex-an-der or San-ti-a-go? Once children catch on, they will all want to take turns being the name-clapper at circle time every day.

2. Dinosaur name-clapping Children seem to have a fascination with dinosaurs. Not only do they like to see pictures of these great beasts in their books or play with toy dinos in the block center, but they love to hear their names pronounced. Get out your dinosaur books for some terrific name-clapping. In *Saturday Night at the Dinosaur Stomp* (Shields, 1997, Cambridge, MA: Candlewick

This girl is making up a story by drawing her version of an ankylosaurus from a toy model.

Press), the dinosaurs all gather for their annual bash. *Ple-si-o-saur-us* paddles in. A *pter-o-dac-tyl* family flies in. A *pro-to-cer-a-tops* brings her eggs. *Dip-lo-doc-us* plods on big fat legs. Mama *mai-a-saur* brings her babies. *I-guan-o-don* shouts. *An-kyl-o-saur-us* drums. *Pen-ta-cer-a-tops* performs. *Ty-ran-o-saur-us Rex* leads a conga line. Even you will be learning how to pronounce these tongue-twisters when you all clap out the dinosaur names.

Follow up if the children are interested with a story re-enactment. Children can make their own dinosaur heads with paper bags. You can print the hyphenated names of the creatures on cards to be worn around the necks of the actors. Now the children can see for themselves what dinosaur names look like when separated into syllables to help them pronounce the names. Converting spoken sounds into written word segments helps children understand more about how speech is converted into writing. Have the actors dance up a storm to a tape or CD with a strong beat.

Some children are sure to want to draw or paint pictures of the dinosaurs. When you or they label their pictures, be sure to hyphenate the names so children can see the syllables. Some children will want to see their own names written in hyphenated syllables like this, too. They may also want to make up their own stories about the Dinosaur Stomp, featuring the character they represented.

REFERENCES

Chapman, M. L. (1996). The development of phonemic awareness in young children: Some insights from a case study of a first-grade writer. *Young Children, 51*(2), 31–37.

Opitz, M. F. (2000). *Rhymes & reasons: Literature and language play for phonological awareness.* Portsmouth, NH: Heinemann.

Roskos, K. A., Christie, J. F., & Richgels, D. J. (2003). The essentials of early literacy instruction. *Young Children, 58*(2), 52–59.

Wasik, B. L. (2001). Phonemic awareness and young children. *Childhood Education, 77*(3), 128–133.

UNDERSTANDING READING PROGRESS . . .

CONCEPT

Children in early childhood classrooms are in the beginning stages of learning to read. As they participate in the playful learning activities you have set up and the book reading and storytelling you have arranged, they begin their emergence into literacy. For you to understand their progress in this emergence, it is important for you to look at each child separately. Learning to read is a complex process that each child approaches individually. Although reading accomplishments can be listed chronologically, not every child progresses in this order, some skip certain steps altogether, and some emerge into reading through writing. Thus, it is essential that you view children's progress one child at a time and that you use several different assessment techniques.

How will you do this? Assessment of children's reading behaviors in the classroom can be accomplished in a number of ways:

- ongoing observations using logs and developmental checklists
- analysis of children's art and writing products
- videotaping and audio taping children at work and play
- individual interviews

Why Assess Reading Behaviors?

It is important to learn where each child stands in his progress of emergence into literacy in order to plan appropriate activities that will support this development. If you find that many of the children have never had experience with books before, you will want to work with small groups doing book-holding and page-turning games. Daily reading to small groups and individuals should be your most important activity. Bringing children together with books should be your goal. A selection of highly attractive picture books and their accompanying character dolls, puppets, or stuffed animals should be available to the children, with each book being a lead-in to various classroom activities (see WEBS). Literacy bags with paperback versions of classroom books can be sent home with the children.

As soon as children and books truly come together, their reading behaviors will change. Thus it is important to keep up your assessment of their accomplishments as an ongoing process. If you find after several months that many of them have not yet developed a "sense of story," you will want to set up activities that help them understand how stories evolve in a sequence of events. Folktales, flannel board stories, predictable books, and story re-enactments should support this growth. A book buddy who already knows what a story is can be paired with a child who hasn't caught on yet.

Pressure to learn should not be applied to anyone, and failure to understand should never be criticized. Children learn at their own speed and in their own good time. Your job is to make books and reading so attractive everyone will want to get involved in the stimulating activities you provide. All the children can take part in every activity. Even accomplished book handlers can participate in the small group that is playing page-turning games. Accomplished story retellers can add immensely to the small group that is still trying to make sense of a story.

ACTIVITIES

1. Start with a reading behaviors checklist. Using the checklist in Figure 45–1 to assess each child's reading behaviors is a good way for you to learn the reading behaviors yourself, so you will know what to look for and expect in the future. The checklist is also helpful for you to determine what activities need to be set up as children progress in their development over time.

This is a developmental checklist describing children's progress and not a list of behaviors that children must accomplish step-by-step, or at all. Some children may have accomplished only a few items. Not many three's and four's will accomplish all of them in preschool. You may also want to keep a daily or weekly log of a child's progress as you note it during the day. This will help you to plan appropriate activities for the child.

2. Analyze children's art and writing products. To determine whether children have developed a "sense of story," look at the series of dated picture-stories (caption pictures) a child has done that you have collected and placed in her portfolio. Do the pictures or captions tell a fully formed story with characters and action, or do the captions mainly label the items in the pictures without forming a story? Check other writing products, such as the child's journal, to see whether a story has been formed. For example, the picture (Figure 45–2) by a 4-year-old boy does not exhibit a sense of story because he is only describing the items in his picture.

In contrast, the caption for the picture (Figure 45–3) by another 4-year-old boy shows that he is beginning to understand what a story is about. He tells what is happening and not only what items are in the picture.

3. Analyze a videotape or audio tape of a child's reading activities, storytelling, or role-playing in dramatic play. As you look or listen to the tapes, can you tell if the child is telling a fully formed story with characters and action or mainly naming things? Is there a narrative with a plot? A beginning, middle, and ending? Sometimes the leader in a dramatic play episode has a story in mind. You may be able to tell this if he directs the other players in what they are supposed to do and

FIGURE 45–1 Reading Behaviors Checklist.

READING BEHAVIORS CHECKLIST

Name_____ Age_____

Observers_____ Dates_____

_____Holds book rightside up

_____Starts with first page

_____Turns pages right-to-left

_____Looks through book carefully without skipping pages

_____Does pretend reading (book babble)

_____Labels objects in pictures (story not formed)

_____Treats each page as separate unit

_____Tells story by naming pictures

_____Understands story is a sequence of events

_____Retells story through memorization

_____Retells story using key story elements

_____Recognizes that print tells story

_____Does finger-point reading of some words

_____Is preoccupied with word recognition

_____Reads print fluently

FIGURE 45–2 "My Sun Has One Eye. All of My Apples Have Legs. This Apple Has Big Hair Because He Eats Good for You Food."

FIGURE 45–3 "The Rain Clouds Made the Rain Come Down and a Rainbow Come Out. The Sun Is Shining Over His House, Cherry Tree With a Red Bird In It, Flower, and a Grape Vine."

Talking about a favorite book helps teachers learn about a child's reading progress.

say. Most dramatic play episodes, however, unfold on-the-spot without much preplanning. Still, you can talk to the players afterward asking them what they were doing and why.

4. Do individual interviews of the children. Neuman and Roskos (1993) say that interviews with children work best when they resemble friendly conversations (p. 258). Because you want the child to respond to your questions giving specific information, sometimes it is helpful to engage the child in an activity which you then ask him to explain. You might have him draw a picture of his favorite learning center, asking him why he likes it or what he does there. Or you might ask him about a favorite book that you can get from the book center, then asking him to point out his favorite character or anything else he likes about the story. Holding and talking about a favorite toy is another way to elicit information from a child in a friendly, informal manner.

Remember, assessment of children's reading progress is for you to be able to set up appropriate reading activities for individuals, groups, and the total class.

REFERENCES

Beaty, J. J., & Pratt, L. (2003). *Early literacy in preschool and kindergarten.* Upper Saddle River, NJ: Merrill/Prentice Hall.

Jalongo, M. R. (2000). *Early childhood language arts* (2nd ed.). Boston: Allyn & Bacon.

Neuman, S. B., & Roskos, K. A. (1993). *Language and learning in the early years.* Ft. Worth, TX: Harcourt.

Owocki, G. (2001). *Make way for literacy: Teaching the way young children learn.* Portsmouth, NH: Heinemann.

UNDERSTANDING SPEAKING PROGRESS . . .

CONCEPT

As mentioned previously, literacy for young children begins with speaking and listening to words. Brain research has shown that a baby's early nonverbal communication efforts help to wire her brain for the spoken and written language to follow. By six months of age, the infant has become a language specialist, focused on the sounds she hears most frequently (Willis, 1998, p. 64). By 20 months of age, children may have a sizable vocabulary—that is, if the adults around her have talked to one another and to her, as well as showing affection and interacting playfully. Children who have experienced little adult interaction or verbal communication are decidedly less verbal themselves. Thus the youngsters who come into your classroom may display a wide range of abilities in their knowledge and use of words. It is your goal to help all children at every level expand their vocabularies and develop confidence in their speaking abilities. Understanding and using words are, of course, the basis for young children's emergence into reading and writing.

What have you accomplished with individual children? Just as you did with children's reading progress, it is important that you make an assessment of children's speaking progress. Although all the aspects of literacy—speaking, listening, reading, and writing—develop simultaneously, it is more expedient to assess them separately. As with reading, it is the observing and recording of individual children's speaking that produces the best evidence of their growth and development.

ACTIVITIES

1. Start with a Speaking Behaviors Checklist. As with reading behaviors, it is important to observe and record a child's speaking behaviors using a checklist like Figure 46–1 to learn the behaviors yourself. Not only will you know what to look for in individual children, but you will be able to make plans for activities to help all children progress in their speaking development.

It is important that you observe each child in your class using this checklist. Reproduce several copies of the checklist to be taped to 3 × 5 cards that you give to staff members to help complete the observations. Start with children who seldom speak. They may speak fluently at home, but are too shy to say much in the classroom. In that case, you will know that the most important activities you can arrange for them will be confidence builders: reading books that feature children's self-concept (see SELF-CONCEPT) and planning activities in which they can succeed and be acknowledged for their success. Using pressure to get them to speak will produce the opposite results. Talk with their parents about how much they are speaking at home and how you are encouraging them to participate in classroom projects. Be sure to mention the positive things their children are accomplishing. If some children seem overwhelmed by the size of the class, pair them with an appropriate book buddy to help them become involved in fun activities two can enjoy.

Sometimes children who seldom speak have a hearing impairment. If you surmise that this is the case, talk with the parents about having their child tested.

2. Make an audio tape of the child speaking to a staff member and to another child, or tape record the child's storytelling. It is important to obtain baseline data, such as a tape of the child's talking, when she first enters the program and later when she has participated in a variety of speaking activities. This will help you to decide which activities are most effective in promoting her growth in this area.

FIGURE 46–1 Speaking
Behaviors Checklist.

SPEAKING BEHAVIORS CHECKLIST

Name _____ Age _____

Observers _____ Dates _____

_____ Listens but seldom speaks

_____ Speaks with single-word answers

_____ Speaks in short phrases

_____ Speaks in expanded sentences

_____ Takes part in conversations

_____ Asks questions

_____ Does chanting, singing, finger plays

_____ Takes roles in dramatic play

_____ Speaks for a doll, puppet, animal

_____ Can make up rhyming words

_____ Can make up a caption story for a picture

_____ Can tell a story from a book

3. Tape record an informal interview you conduct with the child about a favorite book. Analyze the tape you make to see how the child is progressing in her speaking. Does she answer your questions with only one word or with expanded sentences? Can she keep up her end of a conversation with you? Can she make up some funny words for the book character? Some rhyming words? You can serve as her model. Be sure the interview is informal and fun.

From these assessment activities you should be able to interpret what each child's speaking strengths and needs are. Then you will be able to plan activities to support the child's speaking progress. Start from her strengths. If she likes playing with puppets, bring in more puppets and choose one or two other children to play puppets with her. You can tape record their "puppet talk" and play it back for them. Can they make up a story for their puppets? One thing leads to another in early childhood classrooms if teachers keep their eyes and ears open for what is going on with the children. Even shy children eventually respond to activities that involve their special interests.

REFERENCES

Beaty, J. J. (2002). *Observing development of the young child.* Upper Saddle River, NJ: Merrill/Prentice Hall.

Buchoff, R. (1994). Joyful voices: Facilitating language growth through the rhythmic response to chanting. *Young Children, 49*(4), 26–30.

Jalongo, M. R. (2000). *Early childhood language arts* (2nd ed.). Boston: Allyn & Bacon.

Kratcoski, A. M., & Katz, K. B. (1998). Conversing with young language learners in the classroom. *Young Children, 53*(3), 30–33.

Soundy, C. S., & Genisio, M. H. (1994). Asking young children to tell the story. *Childhood Education, 71*(1), 20–23.

UNDERSTANDING WRITING PROGRESS . . .

CONCEPT

As you look at the progress children have made in writing, one thing is sure to attract your attention: every child is different. Some children have trouble holding a writing implement. Others exhibit a strong grip but prefer to draw pictures instead of making letters. A few may create pages of scribble lines, one under the other, without a picture or letter in the lot. It is the same with reading. Some children show little interest in the words in a book but are fascinated by the pictures. It is up to you to plug into children's strong interests and help them progress from there.

When you note that certain children have little interest in reading, but a strong desire to create writing that says something, support them in their quest. They may be the ones who come to reading through writing first. Have them scribble-write what they want to say and read it back to you. Have them scribble-write captions for pictures they have drawn and read them to you. Have them look at large font words in picture books and experiment in writing their own words like that. Have them scribble-write in their journal every day and read it to you. Have them scribble-write responses to your daily messages and read them to you. Children learn to write by writing. When they eventually learn to write words anyone can read, they may suddenly want to read for themselves.

Drawing Can Lead to Writing

Other children may dislike writing but love to draw. Have them draw and draw and draw—all sorts of pictures. You can do the caption writing about their pictures at first if they agree. If they want to communicate something really important in their pictures, as Jenny did in *Patches Lost and Found*, you can help them decide the words to use. Write down a word or two and then ask them for help in what to say. Show them your words. Can they write one of these words?

Because drawing and writing both involve the use of an implement that makes marks, young children often do not differentiate between the two. Both drawing and writing are representational and thus need to be interpreted. Because young children have not learned how to represent all their ideas in words, they often draw pictures instead. Figure 47–1 shows how these drawings can lead children into thinking about writing.

You, too, will need to look at children's drawings and captions to help you assess not only their sense of story, but how they are progressing in the writing process.

ACTIVITIES

1. Have everyone draw/write about a field trip you have taken. Children in one class went on an apple picking field trip and drew picture stories about it afterward. Figure 47–2 shows what 4-year-old Abigale drew. She wrote on the picture after it was finished ("I made a happy apple") and signed her name. Four-year-old Angie also drew first (Figure 47–3), dictated her story afterward, ("Me and my Mommy picking apples."), then signed her name. The class discussion about eating apples and good food gave Kalid a different idea. As he was drawing his picture (Figure 47–4), he told the teacher: "I like to eat strawberries because I don't want to be a candy man." He also signed his name when he was finished.

FIGURE 47–1 How Drawing Leads to Writing.

Note: Adapted from *Early childhood language arts* by M. R. Jalongo, 2000, Boston: Allyn and Bacon. Reprinted with permission.

- Pictures can represent words children do not know how to write
- As children draw they can think about what they want to say
- A series of drawings can motivate them to dictate a story
- Making up a picture caption helps children choose words they may eventually write
- The words they write help children evaluate their picture
- The picture they draw helps children evaluate their words

FIGURE 47–2 "I Made a Happy Apple."

FIGURE 47–3 "Me and My Mommy Picking Apples."

FIGURE 47–4 "I Like to Eat Strawberries Because I Don't Want to Be a Candy Man."

Realizing that Abigale had actually written out her own story made the teacher decide to keep these pictures for later to see if the other children could write out their stories, too. Using caption pictures more than once helps children to take the next step in writing progress. The teacher can then date and interpret these writings for her own progress report.

Figure 47–5 is an observation checklist of children's picture captions to help teachers determine how far along children have progressed in their writing.

Teachers using this checklist to interpret captions from the three previous figures note that in Abigale's drawing (Figure 47–2) she is struggling to write the words ("I made a happy apple") and has crossed out her first attempt. Finally she writes "apple" in upper and lower case letters at the bottom and signs her name A B I g B L E. Her drawing of an apple takes the form of a "head-person" human with arms and hands, an early stage of drawing, as well. Crossed-out or written-over words are a sign of progress in children's writing, telling you that Abigale is aware of the real words, and that she hasn't got it quite right but she is trying. She is in the wonderful transition stage between writing in an "emergent" fashion and "conventional writing." What will it take for her to progress further? More pictures, more writing, and more practice. Be careful not to correct children in this stage as it may shut them down. Let them emerge on their own.

Both Angie (Figure 47–3) and Kalid (Figure 47–4) have not yet progressed to writing their own captions. Or have they? Angie, especially, with her strongly written name and clever illustration, could very well be ready to write her own caption words. Kalid may need more time with his writing, but his imagination has taken off. He also makes a head-person human, but those are wonderful red strawberries with green stems. And is that a chocolate candy bar going into his mouth? (It is brown in the color drawing.) Children who use invented spelling in their captions also indicate that they have developed *phonemic awareness*—perhaps without being taught. Their letters represent the word sounds (phonemes) they hear.

It is so important that teachers give children authentic experiences, expecting and encouraging them to write and draw afterward. But don't let it end there. Read more picture books to them about the experience and use the same drawings to generate more writing and more drawing.

2. Read *Patches Lost and Found.* (Kroll, S., 2001, New York: Winslow Press) Here is a book that is written about a first grade girl, Jenny, but can easily be understood by younger children as well because of the large colorful illustrations and its message.

FIGURE 47–5 Caption Writing Progress.

Name _____ Age _____

Observer _____ Date _____

_____ Child dictates caption to teacher

_____ Child writes linear scribble caption

_____ Child writes letter-like forms

_____ Words are omitted in caption

_____ Words are written over, crossed out

_____ Invented spelling is used in words

_____ Child writes conventional caption

Jenny loves to draw but doesn't like to write. When she has to write a story for homework, she asks if she can draw a picture instead, but the teacher says, "Not unless it goes with the words. Words first!" Then Jenny's pet guinea pig, Patches, escapes and she cannot find him either in the house or neighborhood. Her mother suggests she draw some posters showing Patches and her phone number and place them around the neighborhood. She writes "Patches Lost," along with her number, and papers her neighborhood with pictures. When he doesn't turn up for days, Jenny draws a series of imaginary pictures of a thief stealing him and getting caught by the police. When a man finally finds and returns Patches, Jenny's mother suggests that she write her story under her pictures and take them to school. She does, and her story is a great success, even teaching her teacher that it is okay to do pictures first and then words. For most preschool children, this is certainly the case.

Have your children try drawing pictures of a lost-and-found adventure of their own. Make it fun and funny. Then can they write a few words? You can help. Even a lost-and-found pencil can have an adventure!

REFERENCES

Jalongo, M. R. (2000). *Early childhood language arts*. Boston: Allyn & Bacon.

Neuman, S. B., & Roskos, K. A. (1993). *Language and literacy in the early years*. Ft. Worth, TX: Harcourt.

Opitz, M. F. (2000). *Rhymes and reasons: Literature and language play for phonological awareness*. Portsmouth, NH: Heinemann.

WEBS . . .

CONCEPT

Curriculum webs are devices that assist an early childhood staff in planning learning activities based on a particular theme. Each web is a format for capturing a theme-based curriculum idea as it emerges during brain-storming sessions with the staff and children. Such webs allow the staff to design a program based on appropriate learning goals, interests, and ideas as they occur. The curriculum in many early childhood programs has usually been a previously designed overall educational plan based on an academic subject that the teacher must follow. In contrast, curriculum webs are often constructed on-the-spot and respond to current classroom happenings. Such webs are the basis for an *emergent curriculum* that responds to both the staff's and the children's interests and needs. As Jones and Nimmo (1994) point out in *Emergent Curriculum:* "In early childhood education, curriculum isn't the focus, children are . . . Curriculum is *what happens* in an educational environment—not what is rationally planned to happen" (p. 12).

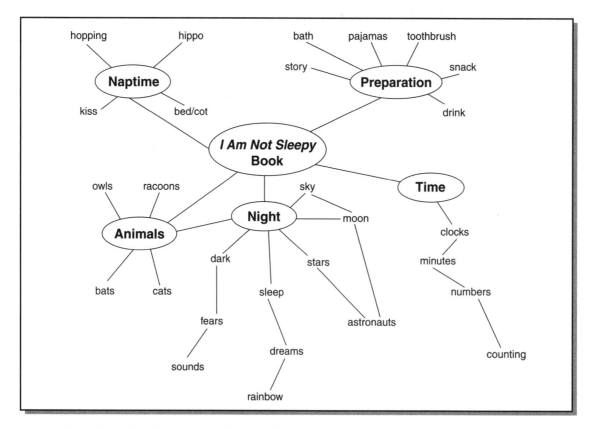

FIGURE 48–1 Web Based on the Book, *I Am NOT Sleepy.*

In a classroom concerned with young children's emergent literacy, such webs will necessarily consist of ideas and activities that support children's development of speaking, listening, reading, and writing skills. The webs presented here evolved from a staff's and children's passionate interest in a particular picture book in use because of a classroom issue it addressed.

The children in this all-day program were having trouble settling down after lunch to take an afternoon nap. One of the picture books the teachers happened to discover that spoke so eloquently to this issue was another Charlie and Lola book like the children's favorite *I Will Never, NOT Ever Eat a Tomato* (Child, 2001). This time the book was called *I am NOT Sleepy and I Will NOT Go to Bed.* The teachers read it during story time just after lunch to try to settle the children and prepare them for a nap. It worked. The children loved it and wanted it read every day. Afterward, they settled down and took their naps. The teachers wondered: with such intense children's interest, could a book like this serve as the focus for other curriculum activities? Here was an opportunity to use the webbing technique to find out.

The teacher wrote the book title in the middle of a newsprint pad and then asked the children and staff to suggest other ideas about going to sleep that they thought about. After each idea she asked what that reminded them of and drew a line from one idea to another, creating the web shown in Figure 48–1.

Next, the staff studied the web to decide what learning centers could involve children in pursuing these topics. They made a second web (Figure 48–2) listing the learning centers and possible activities.

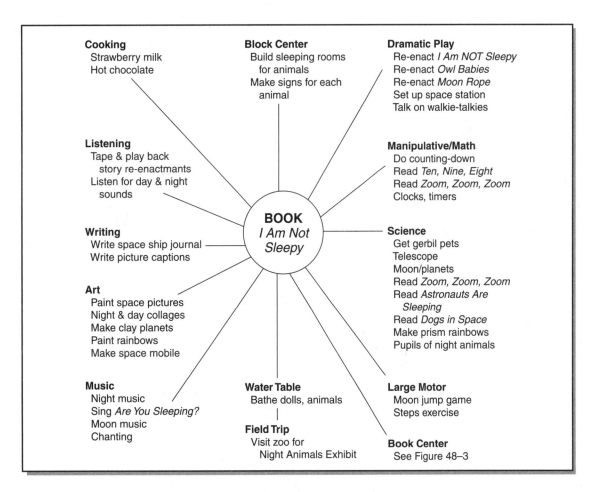

FIGURE 48–2   Learning Center Web Based on the Book, *I Am NOT Sleepy.*

Preparation	**Fear of Dark**	**Moon**
Close Your Eyes	*A Beasty Story*	*Astronauts are Sleeping*
Goodnight Moon	*Close Your Eyes*	*Dogs in Space*
Ten, Nine, Eight	*Francis the Scaredy Cat*	*Goodnight Moon*
10 Minutes till Bedtime	*The Owl Who Was Afraid*	*Moon Rope*
Kiss Good Night	*of the Dark*	*Zoom, Zoom, Zoom, I'm Off to the Moon*
Time/Clocks	**Night Animals**	**Sounds**
10 Minutes till Bedtime	*Owl Babies*	*The Sound of Day, The Sound of Night*
Ten, Nine, Eight	*Stellaluna*	*Hush*
I Am Not Sleepy	*Francis the Scaredy Cat*	
	Dreams	
	Maisy's Rainbow Dream	

FIGURE 48–3   Books to Support *I Am NOT Sleepy* Activities.

Then they searched through their rather extensive library to see what books might support the topics from the webs and came up with the titles in Figure 48–3.

Finally they made lesson plans, one at a time, to support the ideas they intended to pursue (Figure 48–4).

Webs like these can help the staff to focus on children's intense interests and translate them into literacy activities in every learning center in the classroom. Most teachers of young children have learned that one thing leads to another in early childhood programs. Using webs can make these "things" visible and help teachers to decide which of the ideas to follow, as well as how to follow them in the lesson plans they create.

REFERENCES

Beaty, J. J. (2004). *Skills for preschool teachers* (7th ed.). Upper Saddle River, NJ: Merrill/Prentice Hall.

Dizes, D. E., & Dorl, J. (1999). Your mop is my guitar: Emergent curriculum in our classroom. *Young Children, 54*(4), pp. 14–16.

Jones, E., & Nimmo, J. (1994). *Emergent curriculum.* Washington, DC: National Association for the Education of Young Children.

Unit:	**Animals Who Live in the Dark**
Theme:	How can owls fly at night without bumping into things?
Objective:	Children will learn how the large pupils in owls' eyes help them to see at night.
Materials:	A card table and blankets enough to cover it completely; the book: *Owl Babies;* a basket of socks: white and brown; peel-off yellow eye stickers; a black marker; a hand mirror.
Lesson:	Read the story, *Owl Babies,* to one small group at a time. Have them look at the eyes of the three baby barn owls. Do they notice the very large black pupils of their eyes. Talk about the pupils of eyes being the place where light comes into the eyes so we can see. Have everyone look at their own eyes with the hand mirror. Have them notice the black spot in the eye called a "pupil." When it is bigger, more light comes in. Set up the card table and cover it completely with the blankets. Have one child at a time crawl into this dark space and sit for awhile. Talk to the child about what she sees at first. Ask her when she can see more as her eyes get used to the dark. Have her come out and look in the mirror again. Are her pupils larger than before? That means more light can come in and she can see better in the dark—just like the owls. Any child who is afraid to crawl into the dark space may be able to put just his head in under the blanket. If not, don't press the issue.

- Have the children make owl hand puppets with the white socks and yellow peel-off stickers for eyes
- Have them put pupils in the middle of the yellow eyes with the black marker.
- Re-enact the story, *Owl Babies,* with three white hand puppets for the babies and one brown one for the mother.

Are the mother's pupils larger than the babies? What does this mean?

Follow-up:	Read the book, *The Owl Who Was Afraid of the Dark.* Talk about why he might be afraid. How did he get over his fear? Did anyone notice the pupils of the black cat's eyes? What is another meaning for the word "pupil"? Can one word have different meanings?

- Have the children make up their own story about owls.
- Have the children paste a collage of cutout colored paper scraps on black backing paper.
- Take a trip to the zoo to see the night animals exhibit.
- Have children write in their journals about owls.

FIGURE 48–4 Lesson Plan Example for "Animals Who Live in the Dark."

49 WRITING CENTER . . .

CONCEPT

One of the important literacy-focused areas of every early childhood classroom should be the writing center. Such a center can take a number of sizes and configurations. Some writing centers have a scaled-down business desk and chairs, as well as nearby shelves full of writing materials. Others may look like a full-fledged office with a computer, typewriter, phone, filing cabinet, tables for writing, and a bulletin board. Some may take the form of a post office with letter boxes, mail slots, and tables for writing and stamping envelopes. One class made theirs into a newspaper office with desks for the reporters, a typewriter, computer, and stacks of newspapers and magazines. No matter what it looks like, the presence of a writing center says something significant to the children: writing is important in this classroom.

Be sure you fill your writing center with many kinds of writing materials that you change from time to time. Variety is as important to young children as it is to adults. Figure 49–1 shows a number of writing tools and materials.

ACTIVITIES

1. Involve children in using the typewriter. Filling your writing center with supplies is the same as stocking your art center with painting supplies. Make sure the materials are authentic and not children's toy implements. Youngsters want to use real equipment and be engaged in authentic activities. An adult typewriter, for instance, is always preferred to a child's toy typewriter. Old, standard manual typewriters are often available from used office equipment dealers or parents. Although children often play around with a typewriter at first (manipulation), eventually they learn by trial and error to press the keys without jamming them. Letters on the keys become meaningful when they learn to press them one at a time to type their names.

What else can they type? Simple messages are the easiest, although some experienced "typists" will want to write simple stories. Be sure you read to them the comical book: ***Click, Clack, Moo, Cows that Type*** (Cronin, D., 2000, New York: Simon & Schuster), about the cows that find an old typewriter

Pencils	Pens & Markers	Rubber Stamps	Paper
Regulation size	Ballpoint pens	Alphabet letters	Typing paper
Primary size	Felt tip markers	Animal stamps	Notebooks
Colored	Various colors	Address stamps	Stationery
Automatic	Chalk; chalkboard	Colored stamp pads	Colored paper
Pencil Sharpeners		**Miscellaneous**	
Desk sharpener	Paper clips	Glue; paste	Stencils
Hand-held sharpener	Stapler, scissors	Cellophane tape	Stamps
	Hole punch	Peel-offs	Scales

FIGURE 49–1 Writing Tools and Materials.

This busy "newspaper office" is always filled with children occupied with writing on their own.

in the barn and type Farmer Bob a message about being cold and wanting electric blankets. Can your typists type a message (invented spelling is fine) about what they want to do next?

2. Start a sign-making shop. Children who enjoy writing can make signs to be used around the classroom. The block building center, for instance, often needs signs that say Stop, One-Way, Zoo, Please Don't Touch, or Save this Building. Other areas also need label signs saying Dramatic Play, Music, Art, Manipulatives, Water Table, Science, or Waste Paper Here. The book center may need sign-out cards for the books or literacy bags children will be taking home, as well as sign-up clipboards for the computer or tape player. Be sure to read your signmakers the book, ***The Signmaker's Assistant*** (Arnold, T., 1992, New York: Dial) about the boy who creates chaos when he mislabels signs all over town when the real signmaker is away.

3. Put together writing bags full of supplies for home lending. On nearby shelves, you can store plastic bags and cases or backpacks of writing supplies you have assembled for overnight lending. Children can borrow these cases to be used at home and returned the next day just as they do with duplicate paperback picture books that you circulate to the homes. Many parents may not be aware of their children's desire and need to communicate in writing at this early age. Send home some of their classroom writing, as well, and ask the parents to share some of the writing their children do at home. Remember, this should be a pleasurable activity, not a chore or homework.

REFERENCES

Bradley, D. H., & Pottle, P. R. (2001). Supporting emergent writers through on-the-spot conferencing and publishing. *Young Children, 56*(3), 20–27.

Dyson, A. H. (1990). Symbol makers, symbol weavers: How children link play, pictures, and print. *Young Children, 45*(2), 50–57.

Miels, J. C. (2001). Abby Bear deserves to be heard: Setting early writers free. *Young Children, 56*(2), 36–41.

Roskos, K. A., & Neuman, S. B. (1994). Of scribbles, schemas, and storybooks: Using literacy albums to document young children's literacy growth. *Young Children, 49*(2), 78–85.

50 WORDS, WORDS, WORDS . . .

CONCEPT

Words, words, words—what children say, what children hear you say, what children write, what they see written. No matter how you look at it, emergent literacy involves words. To become literate, children need to learn all about words. What have your children learned about words from the strategies you have used with them from this text?

- Can your children identify many words?
- Do they understand that words are made up of letters?
- Do they know that groups of letters make up sounds?
- Are they aware that the words in a picture book tell the story?
- Can they recognize rhyming words?
- What words sound alike to them?
- What "sound words" do they know?
- Do they know any angry words? Any funny words?
- Can they recognize any large font words?
- What words can they write?
- What words can they spell?
- What words can they read?
- Can they read the words on any signs?
- What is their favorite word?

By now, you realize that young children learn best through play. Children already know this fact and begin playing with anything new almost immediately. Playing with words should be no trouble at all for them, but it will be up to you to set up playful activities that teach them new concepts about words. You can have word hunts, word treasure chests, word beanbag, secret words, word surprises, word smelling contests, word missing contests, word eating contests, water word contests, sand word contests, word day contests—and on, and on. Here are a few. Can you also make up some of your own?

ACTIVITIES

1. Word hunt. Names are words that children soon recognize, thus it is more meaningful for them to begin with names. Animal names may be easier at first to recognize than other children's names, so start this game with a card on which you have printed the name of each animal you have in your block building center. Start with short names at first, and set out the animals on a table for one of your small groups: cat, dog, horse, cow, pig, sheep—not too many. Hold up each card, say the name, and have the children place it in front of the correct animal. Now shuffle the cards and try again. Can any of the children say the name on the card? Do this until they really know the names. Now it is time for the word hunt. Take the cards and place them here and there in the block center. Don't make them too hard to find. Stand up the horse and ask the small group to find the name of this animal. Once they have found the correct card, put out another animal and have them find its name.

Another variant of this game is a word hunt with animal puppets. Use big mouth jungle puppets (monkey, rhino, giraffe, alligator, panda, tiger) and hide their name cards in a different learning center. Have each child in your group of six choose and wear a puppet that will have to find its name card. This may be more difficult because the names are longer. Another day, have five children's names on the cards and have the children hide here and there around the room. The sixth child can choose one name card and try to find its owner.

Another day, bring out some of the children's favorite animal books and see who can find a word in a book that matches one of the word cards or one of the animal pictures.

2. Word smelling contest. Do words actually smell? They do when you write a word representing a smell on a card and then place it in a bag along with its smell. For instance, sweet, sour, lemon, onion, chocolate. Open the bag slightly and let one child at a time take a sniff. Once they have identified the smell, pull out the word and let them hold it. The lemon bag can hold two words: sour and lemon. Mix up the bags and let each child try to identify which one her word came from. Put the cards back in the bags and play it again.

3. Word eating contest. Make cookie dough in the cooking center. Then put out short-name animal cards and help children to form letters from the dough to spell the animal name. Put them in the oven to bake and eat.

4. Water word contest. Choose one of the children's favorite books and create a series of word games around it. For instance, one class simply loved the silly words and actions from the book ***Down by the Cool of the Pool*** (Mitton, T., 2002, New York: Scholastic). So the teacher decided to start her word games in the book center with a group of ten children and then move over to the water table. As she read the story, she brought out the animal character mentioned and gave each one to a child to hold: frog, duck, pig, sheep, cat, dog, goat, pony, donkey, and cow. Each of these animals makes its own move in the story:

Frog—dance	Cat—bound	Pony—prance
Duck—flap	Dog—frisk	Donkey—drum
Pig—wiggle	Goat—skip, hop	Cow—caper
Sheep—stamp		

This boy wanted his dinosaur skeletons to be involved in the sand word game. He said they could "clatter"!

Then she read the story again and had each child make the move with his animal. Any move would do. Next time through, they all stood around the water table while the teacher read the story. After each toy animal made its move, the child could toss it into the water table (the pool). After everyone had calmed down and returned to the book center, the teacher challenged each animal holder to find the WORD on the page she was reading that told how their animal moved. Most of the movements are in large font print, children soon discovered.

5. Sand word contest   Ideas like this can apply to any book the children like. Some are sure to want to create a **Dinosaurumpus** (Mitton, T., 2003, New York: Scholastic) where the different dinosaurs donk, bomp, snip-snap, twist, clatter, rattle, twack, and zoom-zoom. This story could be read around the sand table (the sludgy old swamp) with the children holding toy dinosaurs and having them burrow into the sand after they make their moves. The point of all this bizarre activity is not to teach children to identify funny words, but to help them make the connection of words with sounds, and spoken words with written words. In other words, to make words *memorable;* then they become *meaningful.* That is what emergent literacy is all about. Let the children themselves help create your next word game. Good "wording" to you and everyone who reads this!